THE
RETARDED
CHILD

Robert Isaacson, Ph.D.

Argus Communications

Niles, Illinois

To Parents
of
Retarded Children

Thousands of families throughout the world have retarded children. There is nothing unusual about it, except that it has happened to *you*. If it has, you will get all the sympathy you need from friends and relatives. The purpose of this book is not to sympathize with you. You need to face the situation as realistically as possible, to do those things that must be done, and to prepare yourself for the changes in your life that will follow.

There is no going back. Your life will change, it must change, it has changed. How much your life will be affected depends upon the severity of your child's retardation and the other physical or physiological disorders from which your child may suffer. The changes you will need to make in order to meet the new situation will be greater or smaller, depending on your own circumstances, but change must be anticipated and recognized.

Retarded children are often not able to function in a highly technological world of engines, machines, accounting, taxes, computers, and adherence to a time schedule. On the other hand, most are able to be happy, to enjoy the company of others, music, some sports, good food, and friends. Indeed, because of some of their altered abilities they may lead happier lives than most people who are "normal." They will take their pleasures in different ways from most, but also they will not be plagued by the worries about future successes and failures that plague most of us. Their handicaps free them from many of the abstract sources of pain and anxiety troubling modern man.

These remarks should not be interpreted to mean that the retarded individual lives in an idyllic world of pleasure without pain. They have their own fears and concerns, their own anxieties and worries, but, just as with their joys, their fears and worries tend to be somewhat different from those of others. Their mental handicaps affect their ways of dealing with the modern world around them, but do not make them any less human.

CONTENTS

FOREWORD

It is a peculiarity of American life that a person can live his entire life and never encounter someone with a disfiguring skin disease, an amputee, a corpse, or a mentally retarded person. The schools and the mass media do not educate by enlarging our awareness of all that exists so much as they indoctrinate narrow views of reality. All too many people grow older, but they do not grow.

Personal growth, or the possibility of growth, begins with an encounter with what first appears as tragedy. When the world presents us with somebody we did not expect and were not prepared for, we can collapse in helpless despair or respond with new resources that have been evoked by the challenge.

The distinctive feature about this book is not just that it is well and clearly written. Robert Isaacson shows that the encounter with a retarded child is a challenge to grow in the capacity to love someone who appears different from ourselves, but who, on closer examination, is but us in another perspective.

Sidney M. Jourard
Gainesville, Florida
Summer, 1974

PREFACE

"Mental retardation" is a term used to describe conditions of impaired intellectual function. The impairment is such that the retarded person is handicapped in dealing with his or her environment. It represents a lesser degree of the many abilities needed to learn and cope with the requirements of a society in which education is highly valued and required for employment. Most frequently the conditions leading to mental retardation have affected development before, at, or at some time shortly after, birth. However, impaired intellectual abilities can result from accidents or disease in later life and lead to behaviors that are often indistinguishable from those that begin early in life.

Every twenty-four hours there are 140,000 or more people in the world than there were before. This is the amount by which the birth rate exceeds the death rate. Statistically, 3 percent of the population have impaired mental abilities. This means that there are at least 4,200 more retarded individuals in the world today than there were yesterday. Using this same way of estimating, if there are roughly 3.5 billion people in the world, at least 105 million of them are mentally retarded. Thirty-five million of these will be severely retarded. Since there are two parents for every child, there are at least 210,000,000 parents of retarded children. If we assume that there are two other children in the average family with a retarded child, this means that there are over 210,-000,000 siblings of retarded children. So the extended families, that is, the parents and siblings, of retarded children amount to over 420,000,000 people.

More than 3 percent of the population suffer from mental retardation in many regions of the world. The highest rates of population growth are found in the countries with high birth rates and low average incomes. It is in these countries that undernutrition and malnutrition exert their greatest influences. There is little doubt that inadequate nutrition, especially in the first few weeks, months, and years of life, can lead to disturbances of growth and development resulting in reduced intellectual capacity. Other conditions existing in the relatively poor countries can also lead to mental retardation. Of special importance are inadequate prenatal care of the mother and inadequate postnatal care of the infant.

The ghetto areas found in all of the world's major cities make their own special contributions to mental retardation. The diseases, pollution, and poisons of the city ghetto add to the incidence of retardation. For example, many walls of apartments in ghettoes are covered with paint containing lead; lead poisoning leads to retardation. Mental retardation probably occurs twice as frequently in ghetto populations and in underdeveloped countries as in areas of adequate hygiene, nourishment, and medical care. Thus, the figures given earlier are minimal estimates.

Not only is the population growing, but the *rate* of growth is also increasing in many countries. Therefore, the conditions that lead to a high incidence of retardation are becoming exaggerated with every passing day and year. The more widespread they become, the more retarded children there will be. This book is about mental retardation and not about population control; nevertheless, the conditions of overpopulation and economic underdevelopment go hand in hand. Both work together to increase the occurrence of mental retardation.

If you are a parent of a retarded child, you are not alone. Your feelings and thoughts are shared by many others. Your problems are not unique. Other parents have experienced them, faced them, and found ways to make their lives and the lives of others in the family better than they would have imagined. Unfortunately, there are parents who have not been successful. Their lives have become tragic and pitiful. What leads to decisions and actions that make for a satisfactory adjustment? This book reflects some thoughts about these decisions and provides information that may help parents and others approach them in a reasonable fashion.

This book is written for several audiences. The first is made up of parents who have discovered that their child is retarded at the time of the child's birth. The second audience is made up of parents who have learned of their child's problem later in life. The immediate decisions that must be made by the two types of parents are somewhat different, since retarded children of different ages have different sorts of needs and problems. However, the parents of the newborn child with mental deficiency will also have to face the problems presented by an older retarded child in the future. A third intended audience is represented by the friends of parents of retarded children who wish to be more knowledgeable about the problems their friends are facing.

The discovery that a child is retarded sometimes can be made at the time of birth. Children suffering from Down's syndrome (mongolism) and babies with gross neurological or physical abnormalities are cases in point. Yet, even if the physician knows or strongly suspects that a child is retarded, sometimes he does not tell the parents because he does not wish to alarm or distress them. Also, in some forms of retardation the early signs are mild and a wrong diagnosis can be made. Some physicians wait to tell the parents about their suspicions until they can be certain. In still other conditions of retardation the first signs of abnormality do not appear until later in life. It may be months or years, perhaps even into the school years, before the retardation becomes apparent. Is it best for physicians not to tell parents about suspected mental retardation in the early months and years of a child's life? This is, of course, a matter of judgment that must be made by a physician relative to the particular parents in their own individual circumstances. It is, of course, a very difficult thing to learn that one's child is retarded; in general, the diagnosis will be more difficult to accept as time goes by. The love and affection that have been given to the child, and the rewards and gratifications the child has given the parents, will make it more difficult to consider any possibility that the child may not be normal.

In some cases, the parent's awareness of a child's mental retardation comes through persistent health problems or a slowness in learning. Many parents first seek professional help because of a specific problem, such as suspected deafness, poor or delayed speech, prolonged bed-wetting, a general negative attitude, destructiveness, or general withdrawal. After consulting several specialists, at least one of the parents will become concerned over the general development of the child.

Mental retardation is often, if not always, associated with other developmental problems. The same conditions which have led to the abnormal or arrested development of the brain, reflected in the mental retardation, often produce an arrest in the development of other organs. The more severe the retardation, the more likely it is that other systems of the body will be affected. The eyes, ears, heart, and muscles of the body all may show disturbances in growth.

On the other hand, impairments in vision, hearing, or other physical characteristics can occur without being associated with mental retardation. Naturally, it is important to determine whether the developmental problems causing parental concern are due to a specific problem, such as hearing loss, or to a more general arrest in development of which the partial deafness is but one component. When it has become clear that the child's difficulties do not arise only from a specific physical defect, such as deafness, but are associated with some form of mental retardation, it is important to face the problem squarely.

ONE

DECISIONS

This book is intended to provide information about and an honest and forthright orientation to the problem posed by mental retardation. Anything less would be useless and encourage parents to look upon their situation with romantic self-pity.

After learning about the retardation of their child, parents need to make important decisions both for themselves and for the child. These decisions will be critical for their future, for the future of the family, and for the future of the retarded child. They must have a clear view of the effects of their decisions upon all of the people involved.

The parents should become aware of similar decisions that have been made by parents of retarded children at other times and in other places. As possible decisions are investigated, the range of understanding will increase to encompass much more than a single child, going beyond a particular problem to include children with all sorts of developmental defects. Awareness of all the unfortunate conditions of mankind everywhere will be increased.

Let us begin by considering the problems faced by the parents of a child diagnosed as suffering from some form of retardation at birth. If it is possible to make a diagnosis at birth, it is likely that the child will be severely affected, since the developmental problems have been so intense and general as to be detected this early. The abnormality is not likely to be of a subtle nature.

Let us assume that the parents have just learned that their baby is retarded. All decisions will be difficult, since the climate for rational decisions is far from favorable. Unfortunately, now is the time the decisions must be made for themselves, the family, and the child. These decisions cannot be put off. The buck cannot be passed any further. The parents must make decisions. No one else can.

The most immediate decisions are related to what will happen to the child in the next few weeks and months. If the parents have learned about their child's condition while the baby is still in the hospital, there are three options. These are (1) to take the child home; (2) to institutionalize the child, whether in a public or private institution; (3) to place the child with foster parents. Sometimes there is a temporary fourth alternative, namely, asking the physician to keep the baby in the hospital for a few additional days until a decision can be reached. Sometimes it is helpful for the mother to have a few days away from the hospital to study the possibilities, to gain a little time to think. This fourth possibility may not exist if the hospital is crowded. Then the choices boil down to taking the baby home, placing it in an institution, or finding some satisfactory foster-parent arrangement. It is among these three possibilities that a choice must be made.

Steps toward a decision

Naturally, the first thing to do is to search for advice. Advice is easy to come by. Often the first advice comes from physicians—the obstetrician who helped to deliver the baby and the pediatrician taking care of the baby. A hospital social worker, if there is one, will usually visit the mother to discuss the situation. There will be other people with advice and information. These include the family, especially the grandparents; the priest, minister, or rabbi; and perhaps other parents of retarded children. The advice and information received will often be contradictory. How can the sources of information be evaluated?

The best advice possible would come from someone who has had a lot of experience with the problems of retarded children and their parents, who understands the mother and father quite well but who is not so close to them as to be less than objective, who knows the circumstances of the family, and who knows the programs and services for retarded children in the area. There is no one who can meet all of these requirements; therefore, information and opinions from a large number of sources must be distilled and evaluated.

Often some of the worst advice comes from the immediate family. The grandfathers and grandmothers of a retarded child will be just as troubled and upset as the parents. Their experiences with retarded children and with families who have them are usually limited. Their advice will be colored by their own profound emotional stress. The best advice I have heard was from a grandfather who said, "I don't know what to tell you. Go find the *best* professional advice and then follow it." Examples of poor advice include: "Put the child away. Never think of it again!" and "I don't care what those doctors say. There is nothing the matter with that baby."

Other parents of retarded children may also provide some useful information. However, it must be recognized that many of them have not made successful adjustments to their own situations. Also, the decisions made by one set of parents of retarded children may be appropriate for their situation but not for others. It is difficult, if not impossible, for parents who have just learned of their own child's problems to recognize how well other parents have coped with their problem or how similar their circumstances are. Nevertheless, advice from other parents of retarded children is a source of information which cannot be duplicated in any other way. These people have lived through the initial shock, have experienced the problems, and have found at least some resources and agencies of the community from which help can be obtained.*

The best advice can be given by a professional person who is an expert in the behavioral and developmental problems of retarded children. Ideally, this person

---

*The best way to contact parents of retarded children is to call your local association for retarded children. These are county- or city-wide organizations. They will be listed in the telephone directory. Each state has its own statewide association for retarded children, which can also be contacted to learn the names of the officers of the city or county associations.

would be someone who has had many years of experience working with both children and parents. Such a well-rounded expert is difficult, if not impossible, to find. Quite often parents must settle for a person with limited experience. The limitations of the expert must be taken into consideration. Many experts have their own particular biases, which must be considered too.

One possible bias held by some professionals is the opinion that retarded children should be brought home and raised in the family under almost every possible circumstance. They believe that any other decision represents an abdication of parental responsibility. They hold the opinion that placing a child in an institution always produces a permanent and profound deterioration of the child. The possible effects of institutionalization will be discussed later on, but even if one has the most negative feelings towards institutions, there are other factors which must be considered. Of primary importance among these "other factors" are the effects on the parents and other children of bringing the child home. It would be futile to bring a retarded child into the family only to have it exaggerate difficulties already existing in the family beyond the breaking point. Therefore, while placing the child in an institution may have disadvantages, it must be seriously considered. The negative effects of an institution on a child depend upon both the nature of the institution and the nature of the disability from which the child is suffering. In fact, some institutions for the retarded provide warm and loving care along with specialized training programs designed to meet the individual needs of the residents.

On the other hand, other experts are of the opinion that immediate institutionalization is the only sane course of action. They tell parents to place the child in an institution and to resume their normal activities. People with this approach seem to believe in the adage, "Out of sight, out of mind." Still others believe that a child with limited mental potential is a waste of everyone's time. According to them, the best solution would be to place the child in a custodial institution with others suffering from similar mental limitations.

In any case, placing the child in an institution does not lessen the parent's realization of having a retarded child. Putting the child "away" does not allow them to return to life as it was before.

There are certain general principles to be considered concerning the merits and faults of institutionalization, placing the child in a foster home, or bringing him or her home. It is up to the mother and father to weigh the various factors involved to determine how they apply to their own situation. The decision in every case is a personal and individual matter. What works well for some children and for some families will not work at all for others.

Factors to be considered

What sort of influences should bear upon the decision as to where to place the baby? In considering this question from the point of view of parents with a newborn, it should be recognized that many of the same considerations apply to decisions to be made for older children. First of all, there is the matter of personalities, habits, motives, and life-styles of the parents. Related to these are the financial and socio-economic circumstances of the family. All these factors must be discussed by the father and mother, painful as this will be. The views of each parent must be considered and a decision reached which is satisfactory to both. The decision cannot be made by only one parent. Both must participate in the decision, since both must share in the consequences of the decision.

The parents

In extreme cases the father or mother will find it impossible to tolerate the presence of a retarded child in the home. When this is the case, an insoluble conflict between the parents results if the child is brought home. Fortunately, such intense differences between parents over bringing the child home are rare. Nevertheless, there are some families who have reached the brink of disaster because of conflicts in opinion about the placement of the child. Some fathers have just left the home rather than have to see and interact with the affected child. Some fathers come home, but later and later in the evening, seeming to hope that the child will be asleep by the time they arrive. Some mothers drink to escape from the ever-present retarded baby or child. Others develop illnesses that keep them from the usual childrearing role.

It is easy to blame parents who cannot seem to accept the presence of the retarded child, yet it is difficult for people to be different from what they are. Each of us has his or her own unique personality, attitudes, values, and motives. Some of these attributes may not be appropriate for raising a retarded child, even though they may be of great value in other ways. The role of critic is always easier than the role of participant.

To make the best decision, parents must try to step outside themselves and to look at their lives realistically and objectively. They must ask themselves, "What are our long-term goals? What sort of lives do we lead? How important are financial success, social acceptance, doing a 'good job' at work, creating new products or ideas, or enjoying the accomplishments of our other children?"

The parents should not try to decide what their goals in life *should* be, but what they *are*. A retarded child may be a much greater disrupting influence in a family with an intense desire for success in the business or professional world or in terms of social accomplishments than in a family with more modest goals. Further, many mothers and fathers take a special pride in the educational and social successes of their children. For such parents, the realization that a retarded child will have but limited success in these areas must be considered.

Any baby coming into an unstable family situation can be a disruptive influence. A retarded child in an unstable family will be more of a disrupting influence than a normal one, because of the greater care it will require and the fact that it will be a continuous reminder of the dashed parental hopes and aspirations. Therefore, the stability of the family and the marriage should be realistically considered. No child, retarded or normal, can make an unstable relationship into a stable one. A retarded child in the home will magnify the stresses that already exist.

Another factor to be considered is the number of children already in the family and the number of children desired. If there are four or five other children, the addition of one more child, retarded or normal, will not produce the same amount of disruption as the presence of a retarded child when there is one or no other children.

The effect of the bringing of a retarded child into a family situation can be considered in terms of the effects upon the other children. A retarded child takes more time and effort to care for than a normal child. Such a child often has problems with feeding and sucking, is sometimes slower to toilet train, talk, and walk, and is more prone to childhood diseases. The child may also have other medical problems that require attention and time. Where does this time come from? It comes at the expense of the time given to the other children. In general, the larger the family, the easier the transition will be.

Naturally, if the retarded child is first-born, it cannot detract from the attention given to children already present in the family. The danger here is that caring for the retarded child may become an all-consuming project for one or both parents. If it does, the parents may come to feel that they just do not have time to have other children, regardless of their long-time hopes and plans.

The amount of care that a new baby will require depends upon the physical condition of the infant. Many retarded children suffer not only from mental limitations but also from other physical or physiological abnormalities. The precise amount and type of care and attention that the child requires must be evaluated. Different forms of retardation are associated with greater or smaller numbers of physical problems. Some of these related infirmities impose schedules upon the family which may or may not fit into the lifestyles of the parents and other children.

Physicians can give advice about what can be expected in terms of the physical development of the child. Some retarded children have seizures, disorders of movement, feeding problems, or special dietary considerations. What sort of care and treatment will be required in the home? How long need this special care be provided? The parents must ask these questions of the physician directly. A general response is not enough. Parents need specific information. They have to know what to expect in the next few months, in the next few years, and over the course of the next ten years. They need to know what can be expected in terms of the course of the child's development. What sort of complications may arise when the baby catches a cold? Will the child be prone to lung disease, heart disorders, infections, or dental problems? Information about all of these is of great importance. However, despite the fact that most physicians are able to provide relatively good information about the physical development of the child, many are poorly informed as to the behavioral development of the retarded child.

Parents must turn to someone who knows what to expect in the behavior of retarded children. Usually there will be experienced psychologists or social workers in the community. Some may be associated with the hospital or with community agencies that work with developmentally disabled children. Parents should try to find out what to expect from them.

Financial considerations

The physical and behavioral problems of a retarded child cost time and money. The financial aspect of the care of a retarded child is a crass subject, but it is a real consideration for parents and should not be ignored. Basically, the amount of money involved depends upon the nature and the severity of the physical problems associated with the mental retardation and not upon the mental retardation *per se*.

Knowing the cost of the special care, diagnosis, and treatment that will be required for the child is essential. This is why the information from the physician must be straightforward and realistic. Quite frequently physicians do not like to consider what the various procedures will cost the parents. It is painful for them, too. The parents must demand to know exact figures about the cost of medical care, the tests which must be made, the professional consultations, physical therapies, drugs, prosthetic devices, and other procedures as they might be needed. The parents also need to know exactly how much their health insurance will pay in each of these categories of treatment. While it may be that parents cannot afford to place their child in a private institution, it may also be the case that they may not be able to afford *not* placing the child in an institution! For example, parents may discover that the medical and health needs of the child are so great that they could only be provided in a state-supported hospital or institution. The parents must ask whether it is financially possible to maintain the child at home. If the child suffers from heart defects or other physical problems which require continued or intensive medical treatment, it may be that the only way to provide them will be to place the child in a public institution. Many families have discovered that it is just not possible to meet the expenses that would be incurred if the child were to be properly and effectively cared for at home. If financial tensions already exist within the family, they could become intensified with the birth of a retarded child. It is a very fortunate family for whom the financial concerns are irrelevant to their decision.

Most private institutions cost a great deal of money, although some exceptions are to be found in private institutions sponsored by church organizations. The cost of a private institution can run as high as $12,000 to $14,000 a year, although some may be found that cost less—perhaps as little as $3,000 to $5,000 a year. Public state-supported institutions usually cost a good deal less. The exact fee charged by a public institution depends upon the laws of the state. In some states cost of institutionalization is set by a county judge who takes into consideration family income and expenditures. In others the financial contribution made by parents is an entirely voluntary donation. In still others a contract is made between the parents and an agency of the state for services that may include institutionalization. The amount to be paid by the parents is negotiated on an individual basis with the agency.

The costs of a foster home for the child are quite variable, too. They may be as low as $50 a month but usually are higher. Homes charging as low a fee as $50 are those operated by people who are motivated entirely by love of the children they serve. Most likely the cost of a foster home will range from $100 a month and perhaps be as much as $200 or $300 a month.

In some states it may be possible to place a child in a foster home and have complete or substantial payments for this service provided by the state. It is important to recognize that, whatever the costs involved, they will continue over the next several years. In addition, parents are usually expected to pay all of the medical and health expenses of the child, as well as to provide clothing and other necessities.

Private institutions and foster homes cost money, and these costs should be estimated at an exaggerated level rather than the minimal amount. It is far better to overestimate the costs than to underestimate them.

Naturally, the types of disabilities suffered by the child make a difference in terms of the cost involved. Foster homes and private institutions gear their costs to the degree of care and attention that the child will require.

Parents anticipate the cost of having a

baby. These estimates are based, explicitly or implicitly, upon the expenses stemming from the care of a normal, healthy baby. The cost for a retarded child is usually greater. Just how much greater, once again, depends upon the nature of the disability and related health problems. Almost all forms of severe retardation are associated with physical disabilities of a major or minor nature. For example, 60 percent of retarded children also suffer from a form of convulsive disorder, or epilepsy. The cost of the medication required to treat epilepsy is not great, but it does add another continuing item to the budget. Mongolism is associated with physiological conditions that dispose the child toward respiratory disorders. Small illnesses develop into more serious ones; therefore, the child must be watched with care. Even moderately retarded children often have troubles with their eyes or ears, and even minor disorders require attention. Thus, extra expenses are involved.

In addition, many forms of retardation require exceptionally intensive diagnosis and evaluation. These are not free services in most areas. As a rule of thumb, a retarded child will cost roughly twice as much to raise and to care for as a normal child. It is also fair to say that the severity of the retardation is directly related to the presence of physical disorders, and therefore, the more severe the retardation, the greater will be the expense.

The effect upon the child

It is important for the parents to try to anticipate the effects of the different possible situations upon the child. There are limits to a child's capacities which are dictated by the nature of his condition. In recent years it has become clear that the abilities of many retarded children have been underestimated. By using new methods of training and instruction, it is possible for retarded individuals to learn more than had been considered possible before. Nevertheless, there are limits to the development of anyone, retarded or not, which are determined by his physical and mental capabilities. Some, but not all, behavioral deficits may be lessened through special care, attention, and training.

Many children need special training and the help of professional skills that can only be found in hospitals or institutions. It is a mistake to think that all services can best be provided at home. In many institutions there are teams of workers, trained in various professions and with a great deal of experience in working with retarded and physically disabled children, that are able to accomplish some goals far better than can be done in the home. These include speech therapists and occupational and physical therapists. They also are likely to have the specialized equipment necessary for their jobs.

Some children will be but little affected by any type of early environment. Children suffering from the most severe forms of retardation will be least affected by their early environment. A severely hydrocephalic child whose illness is unarrested, for example, will probably be little affected by almost any sort of early circumstances. A mongoloid child, on the other hand, can become quite proficient in social skills. These will probably develop more adequately in a family setting for the first six or seven years of life than they would in most institutions.

The great advantage of the home is in the warm, loving care which it can provide and the extent to which the child will learn the basic skills of life. Two things must be emphasized, however. First, not all homes provide emotionally favorable circumstances for the developing child. If the family setting is not warm and pleasant before the birth of the retarded child, it is not likely to be so afterwards. If one of the parents objects to the child, how will this affect his or her development? Second, many foster parents can provide almost as much loving support as natural parents. Many cottage parents in institutions also provide personal affection and individual care. In addition, the singular care and consideration bestowed upon a retarded child in the home sometimes makes a transition to an institutional setting more difficult in later years. The institutional setting is one in which there is active competition between peers; this may be hard for a child who has led an overly sheltered life.

There are other considerations, too. If the retarded child grows up in the company of normal children, even brothers and sisters, these relationships are quite different from the interactions found among retarded individuals living together. Children can be cruel to each other and especially cruel to those who are "different." The retarded child can be chided and ridiculed by the "normal" children of the neighborhood. He may be shamed into trying games and tasks too difficult for him, and consequently may try to escape psychologically or physically from the challenges of "normal childhood."

In any case, it is important to reach an objective opinion about the possible benefits of home life as compared with a specific institution or a specific foster-parent home. Both short-range and long-term effects must be estimated. Since the effects of an institution or a foster home depend upon the nature of the institution or home, it is important for the parents of the retarded child to find out the sort of care and attention given to the children at the different places available. Reports can be obtained about an institution from social workers, physicians, psychologists, and others acquainted with it. Nevertheless, parents should not be satisfied until they have seen the circumstances under which the children live and have observed the effects of these places upon older retarded children who have been in them for several years. This is part of the research in which parents must engage to make an adequate decision.

The reactions of others

The expectations of friends, relatives, and society in general about retarded children and their families play an important role in the decisions made by parents. Friends and relatives often expect parents to become martyrs. Parents may believe that society expects them to alter their lives completely for the sake of their newborn. Accordingly, they undertake the responsibility of raising the retarded child at home, regardless of the effects on the family, the child, or themselves. Indeed, some parents see the raising of the child at home as a way to gain the respect and regard of other people. Decisions based on such considerations are usually unsatisfactory. The child's best interests are not considered, nor are those of the family itself. While the opinions of others cannot be ignored, it is important to realize the nature of their influence on the decision. Parents should ask themselves, "To what extent is our decision being based on what other people expect of us? How are we being influenced by these expectations?"

Very few people are strong enough to ignore or disregard the opinions of others, either about how they lead their lives or about what should happen to a retarded child. Since they cannot be disregarded, the opinions of others must be recognized. "How will the grandparents react to our decision? How will the neighbors, friends, business associates, etc., view our plans? To what extent will the opinions of these others influence us?" These are the sorts of questions the parents must ask themselves.

Everyone likes to think of himself as somehow independent of the social influences exerted by others with whom we come in contact. Yet, when viewed in an objective manner, our behavior often corresponds to what is expected of us. Try as we will, it is hard to escape the demands of "society."

Other children in the family
The number of children in the family into which a retarded child is born makes a

substantial difference in the amount of time which will be devoted to the new arrival. A newborn arriving into a family where there are four previous children can only expect a certain number of hours of attention because of prior arrangements made by the parents with the other children, implicitly or explicitly. A baby born into an otherwise childless family or a family with only one other child will receive substantially more attention.

In the first few weeks or months many retarded children do not need much more parental time than does a normal child. But, even though the retarded baby does not need it, he usually gets it. In some cases this is because the parents feel that they should exert every effort to make the child advance or develop as rapidly as possible. This produces strain in the family situation. The other children may feel that they are being "shortchanged" by the father or mother and come to resent the "intruder."

The birth of a retarded child does not justify ignoring the other children who have a legitimate demand to the time and attention of the parents. The parents' decision must be based in part upon their previously existing relationships with the other children and estimate of the extent to which these will be disrupted or changed by the new child. The family circumstances must be carefully examined in terms of the time available for the care and attention to the retarded baby. At what cost to the other children will this extra attention be paid?

In families with a large number of children, some of the older children are able to help care for new arrivals. This is true for a retarded baby as well. In general, older children like to take care of babies. To some extent, of course, the physical or physiological disabilities of the child, if any, will play a part in how much the older children will like to help take care of him or her.

Family difficulties may develop over the degree of responsibility given to older brothers and sisters for the care of the retarded child. If the demands placed upon the older children are considered by them to be excessive or seem to be unreasonable departures from past responsibilities, the older children may come to resent the retarded child. This is felt most keenly by older sisters, who, by the nature of our society, are most often asked to help around the house.

It is obvious, of course, that not all brother-and-sister relationships are loving and supportive. Just because the older children are siblings of the baby does not mean they will like the new arrival. Some retarded children, because of their deformities, are less lovable than normal children. The extent to which the baby is deformed or retarded *does* make a difference, both to the parents and to other children. It should be recognized, however, that if the child exhibits deformities or behavioral problems that make him difficult to like, there is no reason to believe that the initial response of the family will be permanent. Often, as the other children grow older, they come to appreciate the retarded child despite his physical or mental limitations. However, it may take a considerable degree of time for this affection to develop.

The actual sources of inconvenience produced by having a retarded child in the home vary from one family to the next. However, there are some general points of agreement among parents of retarded children. One study was conducted of a large number of such parents. The following difficulties were frequently mentioned:

1 Family activities were limited.
2 The child required constant supervision.
3 There were additional financial expenses.
4 The mother was often exhausted.

5 The child needed a lot of attention at night.*

All of these are real sources of difficulty for the family. They are felt more or less strongly by all families. They should be considered and evaluated in terms of each individual family situation.

Some of the objective factors that go into a decision concerning the immediate placement of the child have been mentioned. Little more can be said about the home setting, since each is so different from the next. The parents must look at their own circumstances as objectively as possible, considering all of the factors mentioned above, and including any other unique characteristics. However, it may be worthwhile to consider the general nature of institutions and of foster home settings in greater detail.

Institutions

Private institutions are generally not among the possible alternatives for most families because of the high costs involved. However, it may be possible to find some whose costs are within an acceptable economic range in some regions of the

---

*Holt, K. S.: "The Home Care of Severely Retarded Children," *Pediatrics* 22 (1958): 746–55.

country. As mentioned before, many of these are associated with churches and charitable organizations. To determine whether or not there are any such private institutions in an area, calls should be made to the business offices of the larger churches. The Roman Catholic Church often maintains schools for the retarded; information can be obtained by calling the administrative offices of the dioceses. Parents should not hesitate to inquire about institutions run by a particular religious denomination if they do not themselves belong to it. Most often institutions are open to children of parents from all faiths.

It will come as a considerable surprise to learn that there is no single organization or group within any community that has complete information about all of the services available for the retarded child. This means that the parents will have to make a large number of inquiries concerning possible private institutions or programs. Most parents' reaction is to think that there *must* be someone who knows *all* about the services available. Yet I doubt if there is a single locality in which a comprehensive information service is available. The reasons why information is so scattered among the various agencies and groups involved is difficult to understand. Nevertheless, with each phone call and letter new suggestions and new potential opportunities will present themselves.

Public and private institutions vary in quality of care and in the attitudes held by the staff toward the children. Some institutions for retarded children are medically oriented; others are educationally oriented. Some institutions are little more than custodial agencies, which vary only in the degree of efficiency with which they are run. In others there is an active training program developed for every resident. These are often under the direction of teachers and educators. The quality of the institutional programs of state-supported institutions varies not only among states, but within the institutions of a single state.

There is no substitute for a personal investigation of the institutions that may be available to the child. It is possible to arrange a visit by contacting the institution. The visiting parents are usually shown the facilities by a social worker, often on a more or less routine basis. It is important to examine the institution for many different things. These include cleanliness; the quality of the physical structures; food and food service; the educational and training programs (and how many children are enrolled in them); the quality and number of attendants, nurses, and physicians available. Above all else, the prevailing attitude of the employees toward the children should be estimated.

It is critical to know whether the institution will offer sufficient opportunities for a child to grow and develop, become trained and educated, be loved and cared for. It is possible to have all of these opportunities in a spotless and tidy institution, but it is also possible that a spotless and tidy institution is one that is run by such strict rules and by such uncompromising personnel as to allow little freedom for play or creative activities. It is possible to keep a penitentiary spotless by continuous confinement of the prisoners to their cells, and it is possible to keep an institution for the retarded spotlessly clean by restricting the activities of the children.

Public institutions have been troubled by an inability to obtain enough funds to be run the way most of their administrators and staff would like. The salaries of aides are often about at the level of jailers', and both are underpaid positions. Under these conditions, only if there is an enlightened administration in the institution can employees who like the children and who are willing to work with them be recruited and retained. Because of an increasing public interest in the conditions of the retarded and because of recent court decisions, more public funds are being provided to the institutions than ever before. In most states, the funds provided by the legislatures are still inadequate. In overall perspective, however, it can be anticipated that the quality of services provided by institutions will be improving.

Good and bad reports can be obtained about any public institution. It is a mistake to put too much faith in these rumors. The institution has to be seen firsthand. If possible, parents should go to the institution and talk to the staff. They should refuse to be rushed through and should ask to examine areas that may be off the beaten path for most visitors. They should see how the children are served their meals. They should find out what the children do in the mornings and in the afternoons, and how they are put to bed. What happens when the child has a fever, a cold, an accident? The quality of a program can only be judged on this basis of how it relates to children with different degrees of retardation. Each type of retardation needs different kinds of educational, training, medical, and health services. The institution should be judged on the basis of whether or not it fits the needs of the children being served. The same type of approach must be used in regard to examining a foster-parent setting.

Foster homes

Foster parents are simply people who have, for one reason or another, elected to take children who are not their own into their home. They often care for them as they would their own children. Some couples do this because they like to have children in the home. Perhaps they cannot have any of their own or perhaps their children have grown up. Some of these couples recognize the need for the special care required by retarded children and have elected to have only retarded children with them. Other couples approach the matter more from a business point of view, including some who recognize the need for specialized care for retarded children and have worked out a system whereby they can care for two, three, or even more retarded children in their homes. They have established a routine which, in some ways, approximates that which would be found in benevolent institutions. Such homes are really little more than small private institutions. Some foster parents also have children of their own living at home. This *may* be a benefit to the foster retarded children. Unfortunately, there are a few foster parents who have only a commercial attitude toward the care of retarded children. They are interested in them strictly for the money involved. As a result, the foster children may be neglected.

Some foster parents love and care for the retarded children as much as they do their own children; others do not. Once again, there is no substitute for firsthand observation. It is essential to talk to the family involved, both husband and wife, to see the home in which the foster children are cared for, and to make some estimate of the motives of the foster parents. Reports and rumors are not adequate.

In some regions foster homes are under the control of one of the governmental agencies. In such cases it is possible to get a list of approved foster homes that will accept retarded children from the agency involved. In each area it is necessary to determine the agency in charge of regulating and supervising foster homes.

Governmental agencies in different areas exert widely varying degrees of supervision of foster homes. In many areas a social worker visits the homes periodically to inspect their cleanliness and the care of the children. Reports are made to the directing agency and the parents about the home and about the progress of the children. In other regions, the supervision of the foster home is on a voluntary basis, and probably there are some foster homes without inspection or supervision. Even in regions with extensive visitation and evaluation programs, firsthand observation by the parents is important.

The needs of the child

Parents must investigate for themselves the private or public institutions, as well as the foster homes, that might be available. Their evaluation must be on the basis of what the retarded child needs.

A retarded child needs much the same sorts of things as a nonretarded child. Retarded children need love and security. They need attention. They need environmental stimulation. But, in addition, there may be special considerations over and beyond those of the normal child. These include special medical, psychological, or educational diagnosis and treatment. Often these children need an unusual amount of training in simple habits such as eating and toileting. In addition, fostering relationships between the retarded child and other children in the family and in the neighborhood may require special effort. Parents must ask themselves whether or not the institution or the foster home under consideration is going to be able to provide an adequate amount of the experiences that the child will need.

Parents need to be prepared for the special problems that arise during the development of a retarded child. They should be made aware of how a retarded child's growth may differ from that of a normal child. They need to know what to expect from a physical and from a behavioral point of view. They must be able to accept the child's limits and tolerate his behavioral difficulties. They need to be stable enough to resist the unreasoned opinions of their families and friends and to reject inappropriate advice. In addition, the family of a retarded child must face its own personal problems to ascertain whether there is sufficient strength to deal with the problems posed by the child.

It is quite likely that parents will feel more or less overwhelmed by the number of things which must be done and by their urgency after the birth of a retarded child. Nevertheless, the problems will not go away. There is no one to whom the burden can be shifted.

All of the possible alternatives in regard to the placement of a child cannot be explored in the few days after birth. A thorough investigation of all opportunities will take time and effort. In the months and years after the birth of a retarded child, the parents will want to investigate possibilities that they had insufficient time to investigate after the child's birth.

The conditions of the child and the family should be reappraised continually. The immediate decisions are not irrevoc-

able or permanent. The family's circumstances may change, as will the needs of
the child. As unforeseen problems, difficulties, and needs arise, changes in the
original decision may be required. When
new opportunities present themselves,
parents should be ready to take advantage
of them. As with life in general, most opportunities present themselves to those
who are prepared for them.

TWO

FIRST
REACTIONS

When parents learn that their child is retarded, a series of intense and prolonged emotional reactions begin, regardless of how long after the birth of the child this takes place. Every member of the family will be affected. The emotional reactions may manifest themselves in many ways: through physical disorders, mental problems, disruptions of family life. The emotional reactions will be so strong that it is almost certain that the lives of the father and the mother will be disturbed. It is a crisis in both their lives, and personal crises of all kinds result in reduced capabilities of mind and body. Physical or mental problems may develop and last for months. These effects should be anticipated, and it would be wise to consult a psychiatrist or a clinical psychologist shortly after the birth of a retarded child, not for an evaluation of the child, but to help the parents and to minimize the crisis-induced reactions.

The emotional reaction

The reaction of parents to learning that their child is retarded can be described in terms used to describe reactions to any form of stress: (1) an initial "alarm response," and (2) a phase of "resistance." These two initial reactions can be followed (3) either by recovery or by exhaustion.* If recovery does occur, often people come to an emotional adjustment that is more stable and rewarding than that existing before the birth of their retarded child.

During the period of the alarm response, the parents will be in a state of shock, disbelief, panic, and anxiety. All of the emergency reactions to stress are activated. These include a search for some mode of action that may reduce the crisis or its impact. In this first phase any kind of organized action or thought is practically impossible. As the individual's defenses strengthen, however, the second phase is entered. The person is no longer overwhelmed and becomes mobilized to fight off the stress. In this period decisions can be reached and action taken. If, however, a person does not develop a truly

*This terminology is borrowed from that developed by Dr. Hans Selye to describe the body's reaction to stress. See Selye, H., *The Stress of Life* (New York: McGraw-Hill, 1956).

effective adjustment to the situation, the stage of exhaustion will be reached. The third stage resembles the first in many ways. Shock, disorganization, and panic return. A total mental or physical collapse of the person can result.

Very little can be done about the first stage of the reaction. The alarm response occurs, but usually it does not last very long: a few days or a week. It is so intense that it cannot continue long. If the alarm reaction is too catastrophic for one or the other of the parents, it may be possible for a physician to prescribe a tranquilizer or institute other procedures to help bring the emotional reaction within reasonable limits.

The second stage, the phase of resistance, then begins. It is during this second stage that the first steps can be made toward a decision about placement of the child, toward new means of coping with the situation, toward finding new, appropriate life-styles. Parents must take advantage of this resistance phase to initiate action. Solutions, even temporary solutions, will help reduce the stress.

The psychological aspects of the resistance phase of the stress response are constructed out of processes called *defense mechanisms* by psychotherapists. Defense mechanisms help shape and color the behavior of all those deeply concerned with the retarded child. They are responsible for certain behaviors that may seem irrational or peculiar when considered by outside observers. Some understanding of defense mechanisms and how they influence those people who have been deeply affected by the retarded child is important for understanding the second stage.

Defense mechanisms

In the psychoanalytic theory developed by Sigmund Freud, defense mechanisms are thought to be defenses against anxiety. The birth of a retarded child into a family produces very great and serious anxiety for many reasons. Defense mechanisms are mobilized to defend against anxiety from all sources. The defense mechanisms are not mobilized against the events that cause the anxiety but against the anxiety itself. The use of defense mechanisms is not a sign of mental abnormality. Everyone uses them to reduce anxieties arising from any number of experiences when things are just too much to bear. Mental disorders are associated only with the excessive use of one or more of the defense mechanisms to such an extent that they impair the activities of the person in his daily life. In general, however, most people use some defense mechanisms, singly or in combination, to cope with the anxieties of everyday life.

Defense mechanisms operate below the level of consciousness. We cannot select or control them. They occur "automatically." The defense mechanisms produce behaviors that may not seem to be logical or rational ways to deal with the objective situation. But the goal of these mechanisms is to reduce anxiety not to alter the real world. Some work better than others in terms of our overall ability to get along. The behaviors caused by some of the defense mechanisms are not considered unusual, but the more primitive the defense mechanism, the more likely it is that other people will consider the observed behaviors bizarre.

Perhaps the simplest, most primitive of all the defense mechanisms is *denial*. In its most extreme form this defense mechanism accounts for the flat-out verbal denial by a parent that a child has been born. In a slightly modified version, parents often refuse to accept the fact that their child is retarded. If the mechanism of denial works, anxiety will be reduced because the cause of the anxiety has been "eliminated." This is an example, perhaps, of the simple observation that people often fail to see what they do not want to see. This mechanism is so primitive and results in such unusual behaviors that it tends to be used only under the most pressing of circumstances, namely when anxiety is extremely high. Imagine a mother still in the hospital maintaining that she had not given birth to a baby! Denial cannot work for very long. It does not aid the person in adjusting to the situation or to other people. Sooner or later it is bound to fail, and its continued use creates even further anxiety. It is strictly a stop-gap measure. If it is used for a prolonged period of time, active therapy must be undertaken.

The mechanism of denial requires a vast amount of psychological energy. Since the psychological energy required to maintain a defense mechanism must be appropriate to counteract the force of the anxiety, the use of denial as a defense mechanism means that the experienced anxiety is very strong. The greater the energy used to maintain a defense mechanism, the more resistant it will be to change. This is one reason why parents often will continue to deny that there is anything the matter with their child, even in the face of obvious evidence to the contrary. At an unconscious level such parents are firmly committed to the use of the denial mechanism and have very little ability to alter their behavior. Strong support and guidance is required to do so. This is usually best provided by a professional therapist. As time goes on, however, there usually will be a time when the anxiety level has become reduced sufficiently so that other, more efficient, defense mechanisms may be employed.

A mechanism associated with denial is *repression*, which refers to an unconscious rejection of memories. The person does not deny that a particular event or condition has happened; rather, it is forgotten and held submerged below the level of awareness. A commonplace example is that people tend to forget their dental appointments with great regularity. Because of the pain that may have been associated with visits to the dentist in the past, the anticipation of going to the dentist is anxiety-producing. Therefore, as the time approaches, the appointment may be repressed below the level of awareness. The fact that dentists call their patients either the day before or on the day of the appointment to remind them of it is a tacit recognition of this mechanism. In the case of parents of a retarded child, many aspects of the situation, including the child itself, can be pushed out of awareness, forgotten for longer or shorter periods of time. The difference between repression and denial is that when the mechanism of repression is used, material *can* be brought back into awareness, whereas when the mechanism of denial is used, it is as if the event never occurred.

Sometimes the basic defense mechanisms of denial and repression are assisted by supplementary devices. For example, the stressful event may be considered entirely from an intellectual point of view, without any expression of emotion. This mechanism is sometimes called *isolation*. The objective facts are accepted, but the emotional feelings associated with them are denied or repressed. When this mechanism is used, the parent may be able to talk about the condition of his child, perhaps to discuss it in conversation with other people, but he or she will express or experience very little emotion. The emotional reactions are held captive beneath the surface.

In a sense, isolation is an effective mechanism when a parent is dealing with other people. Neighbors and friends may seem surprised and perhaps even admire the way the parent is "taking" the event. The disadvantage of the mechanism is that it requires a great deal of psychological energy to hold the emotions and anxieties out of consciousness. There may be very little energy left for normal activities. There also may be a general flattening of all the emotions. This defense mechanism represents a way in which the birth of the retarded child can be recognized at a verbal or cognitive level while the person is insulated from the great and intense emotional reactions that are naturally associated with it.

A defense mechanism involving the entire individual is called *regression*. This defense mechanism is one in which a person retreats to a form of behavior that is suitable to earlier periods in his life. Often the retreat is back into a style of behavior appropriate for the teen-ager or even the young child. If the regression is so extreme as to carry the person back to periods of his life where there were few, if any, responsibilities, and if behaviors that are clearly childlike occur, professional help may be needed. If the regression is to a period in life that was one of reasonable maturity, the regression may be relatively hard to detect. In essence, the person is moving back in time to a former way of life when adjustments were easier to make.

As an example, a housewife with several previous children who has a retarded child may regress in ways that some people might find charming. She may become ebullient and joyful, engaging in all sorts of recreational activities for which she has not found time in many years: ice skating, roller skating, sledding, or skiing. A careful observer might note, however, that she lets many of the household chores go by the board. By watching her carefully, it might become clear that her behavior is appropriate to a girl of thirteen or fourteen who is a teen-age baby-sitter but not appropriate to being a mother. She may be an excellent baby-sitter, but she may fail terribly at being a wife and mother. By regressing, however, she may have gone back to an earlier time at which it was possible to cope with life.

The defense mechanism of *projection* is one that occurs rather frequently in normal adults. It is often used in conjunction with other defense mechanisms, such as denial. Emotions and desires are projected onto other people. If an impulse to kill, destroy, or hate someone is unacceptable, it may first be denied by the person feeling these impulses and then projected onto someone else. The result is that, instead of the person's being aware of his own hostile feelings, he attributes them to others. "I hate X" is translated into "X hates me." Many people have feelings of dislike and even hatred toward their retarded child just after birth. The birth of the defective child may be seen as a threat to the parents, a disruption in the pursuit of their life goals, and even misinterpreted as their own failure. The conditions, therefore, are ripe for use of the mechanism of projection, but the projection of hostile and aggressive impulses onto the child is very difficult. A baby is, after all, just a baby. It is not easy to accept the idea that the baby hates or is being aggressive. Therefore, the parents' underlying hostility toward the child cannot be turned around to express the view that the child hates them. One solution to this problem is for each parent to use the other as the source of the hate. Therefore, the hate of one parent toward the child is turned about, to be seen as stemming from the other parent. "My husband (or wife) has hated me ever since the baby was born." This type of irrational emotional response does not help produce a stable family situation, obviously.

Reaction formation is a complicated defense mechanism in which unacceptable impulses and feelings are altered to make them acceptable. This is done by reversing the nature of the impulse or feeling. In other words, instead of a person's feeling that he hates and wants to kill another, he feels that he loves this same person. Using an example found in many textbooks of abnormal psychology: if a son's impulse to kill and overthrow a dominant father is unacceptable (the traditional Oedipus complex), this can be translated into the feeling, "I just love my wonderful father," by the process of reaction formation. There is often a clue as to when reaction formation occurs. This is the intensity of the feeling. Feelings resulting from reaction formation are often exhibited in an unusual and inappropriate degree. Often it is like saying, "I love my father to pieces." The "pieces" are really interpretable in terms of the tiny little segments that might result from the father's being hacked to death. Or if a person is "smothered with love" by feelings arising from reaction formation, the smothering may be like suffocation. In short, the translation of hostile and aggressive feelings into affection and love to make them acceptable by the process of reaction formation exaggerates the feelings of love and affection beyond normal limits. They can also be recognized by their unqualified nature. Most normal interpersonal relationships, whether they involve a father or mother, husband or wife, are mixed. There are certain aspects of the other person that are loved and admired, but no one is perfect, so there are qualities of the other person that produce mixed reactions. The overall balance may be toward love and affection, but the point is that our feelings are mixed toward everyone of significance. When there is no such mixed quality, the emotion may be a product of reaction formation.

If a parent does feel hostile, aggressive, or resentful toward a child, whether he be normal or retarded, these feelings may be unacceptable. "What sort of a person would not like a child?" the parent thinks. He or she may evince incredible amounts of love and affection for the child. When describing his or her feelings toward the retarded child, the mother or father will be uniformly positive. Little, if anything, will ever be said about the inconvenience the child may be causing. Other people's negative reactions to the child may be seen as threats to what ought to be a fundamental attitude of love, affection, and acceptance of the child.

It might be thought that the "love" developed by the reaction formation mechanism is an admirable and wonderful characteristic, one that all parents should have. This is far from the case, however. The excessive demonstration of affection resulting from reaction formation is not helpful to the developing child. The child can be harmed by overprotection just as much as by open hostility and aggression. He or she is being overwhelmed, overprotected, and overloved. The real feelings of the overly affectionate parent whose actions are produced by reaction formation can be inferred from the unfortunate effects upon the child.

These are some of the ways in which the individual can respond to reduce the anxiety of a situation. Some of them work reasonably well, so that necessary decisions can be made and an adjustment of the family begun. Some defense mechanisms work better than others and are more easily tolerated by society. For the most part, all of them are temporary expedients. More adequate resolutions of the problem must be undertaken.

On the other hand, defense mechanisms are probably necessary, since there is no simple solution to the difficulties that must be faced by the parents of retarded children. Parents must realize all the aspects of the situation with which they are confronted. One component of the situation is the parents' feelings for the child. Therefore, it is important to make every effort to reduce the use of defense mechanisms and to establish an honest emotional foundation for the future growth of parents and child.

Stage three: exhaustion

Just as the body uses its energies to defend itself against infection and disease, energies are expended to mobilize against anxiety. If the stress of disease continues long enough, the body's energies, which provide resistance to the disease, will become depleted. The third stage of the stress response will be entered. If the parents' adjustments to the birth of a retarded child are not adequate, even the energy required to maintain the defense mechanisms may become drained. The third stage, that of exhaustion, can develop. There is no energy left to support any constructive activity. At the end, exhaustion can lead only to depression and even to death. The mind and body are depleted.

Personal crises and stress weaken physiological as well as mental capabilities. Quite often one or both of the parents develop various types of physical symptoms and diseases after the birth of a retarded child. These may begin soon after they learn of the child's condition or not until months later. These physical complaints are sometimes considered to be "psychosomatic illnesses," but this label does not make them any less real or intense. The fact is that any personal crisis is a stress applied to the individual that results in a reduced ability to fight off infections, to withstand damage and strains, to repair the body. Any disease or disturbance that would normally be easily handled by the body's physiological defenses can now become debilitating. The disruption of the body's physiological mechanisms can be reflected in aches, pains, muscle spasms, stomach disorders, ulcers, indigestion, heart murmurs, colitis, and so on. Minor infections become major problems. Any illness becomes aggravated into proportions that make it a source of medical concern.

Being physically sick can be a concrete step toward a condition in which there is less stress. If a person is sick enough to go to bed or to be admitted into the hospital, then he or she is removed from many of the circumstances producing the stress. This is a way of escaping from the immediate situation. Naturally, it is a short-term approach, but it may be necessary. The stress and anxiety may have built up to a point where it is imperative for the person to get away, to gain time in which to remobilize resources.

Guilt
One of the major factors contributing to the stress and anxiety being suffered by the parents is guilt.

Retarded children are born to many normal couples for unknown reasons. There is nothing the parents could do to prevent the retardation. The only time parents should feel guilty is when their decisions are influenced by factors that are not important to them, their family, or their child.

In most cases, retardation results from an arrest in the development of the baby before birth. In any case, the brain and other organ systems of the body are arrested at some early stage of development. Little is understood of the reasons behind arrested brain development. The abnormally developed brain can be smaller than normal; it can contain fewer nerve cells, or the cells can be differently assembled. The biochemical systems of the body and the brain may also be inappropriately constituted. In some types of retardation an enzyme system important for some aspect of brain function seems to be left out of the organism. In other cases the deficiency of an enzyme allows the production of chemicals within the body that act as poisons to the central nervous system.

There is no doubt that genetic influences play a role in the inheritance of some forms of mental retardation. This is true in some relatively rare forms of retardation, such as amaurotic idiocy, which apparently follows a simple recessive inheritance pattern. The origins of amaurotic idiocy have been traced to a genetic accident (mutation) occurring in a small area of northeastern Poland or southern Lithuania.

The most thoroughly investigated cause of retardation is the small extra chromosome that is found in the cells of mongoloid children. Today mongolism is sometimes referred to as "trisomy 21." The number "21" refers to the name of the pair of chromosomes affected by this disease. There should be two such chromosomes. In the mongoloid child there are three. A set of chromosomes from a mongoloid child are shown in the figure on pages 56-57.

It is possible to inherit an additional chromosome larger than the relatively small chromosomes named "21." In general, babies that inherit an extra large chromosome tend to be aborted. However, people are sometimes found with three larger chromosomes instead of two. If there are three 17 or 18 chromosomes instead of two, the child has malformed ears set low on the head and mental retardation. If an extra 13, 14, or 15 chromosome occurs, the result is mental retardation, eye defects, and cleft lip and palate. These two abnormal genetic conditions are examples that go against the general rule that additional chromosomes larger than 21 will cause the fetus to be aborted.

Individuals may also have additional chromosomes of a smaller size. Cases in which people have one or more additional sex chromosomes have been described relatively frequently. Mental retardation is not necessarily associated with the presence of these additional, smaller chromosomes. This is not to say that these additional chromosomes are without effects upon the individuals involved. There is a possibility that additional X chromosomes are associated with tallness and a tendency toward aggressive behavior.

Mongolism is not a disease entity that

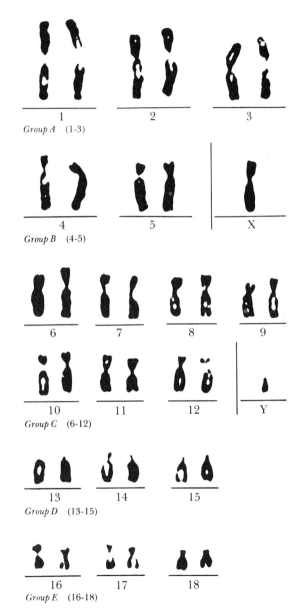

Group A (1-3)

Group B (4-5)

Group C (6-12)

Group D (13-15)

Group E (16-18)

Chromosomes of mongoloid boy

*The original collection of chromosomes is
shown in the circular cluster
of chromosomes. These same chromosomes
have been sorted out on the basis of size
in the rest of the illustration.
Group G in the lower right corner should
have only four chromosomes, two 21s
and two 22s. As can be seen, there
is an extra chromosome in this group,
indicated by the arrow. This is thought
to be a third 21 chromosome, thus
providing the basis for calling mongolism
"trisomy 21." (Chromosome karyotype
courtesy of Dr. Jaime Frias, Department of
Pediatrics, University of Florida.)*

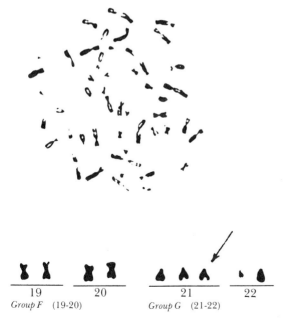

19   20   21   22

Group F   (19-20)   Group G   (21-22)

tends to perpetuate itself. Many male mongoloids are unable to produce sperm or to sustain an erection. Many females suffering from mongolism cannot adequately produce children. If mongoloids seldom reproduce, why is mongolism so prominent a cause of retardation? For unknown reasons, the division of chromosomes in normal people does not always proceed adequately. One child in every 500-600 births is a mongoloid. Most parents of mongoloid children are genetically normal, although there are rare instances in which one of the parents is a carrier of the abnormality. (This possibility should be investigated by parents of a mongoloid child as soon as practicable after the child's birth.) There is some evidence that males may produce sperm with abnormal chromosomes that may cause eggs to engage in abnormal cell division after fertilization, but this possibility is not agreed upon by all geneticists.

Even though several forms of mental retardation result from abnormalities in genetic materials, this should not make anyone feel guilty about causing the retardation of a child. It would be like someone feeling guilty because his heart skipped a beat. A person does not feel guilty about having a physiological condition in which the body's enzymes are inappropriately made, as in diabetes mellitus. All our bodies work in different ways at different times. This is the nature of the biological organism. Nevertheless, some parents feel profound guilt because their bodies operated in some unknown way to produce a condition of retardation in one of their children. This feeling is completely inappropriate.

Guilt may arise from an unfounded belief that the parents have somehow failed. They believe that if they had done something or not done something else, they would not have had a retarded child. All parents have these feelings to a greater or lesser degree. Many parents would not accept the genetic "credit" for the birth of a strong, healthy, and normal child, but it is just as great a mistake to claim a personal responsibility for having a normal child, a genius, or a retarded child. All are accidents of genetics beyond the control of either parent. To use an analogy with a card game, every child is dealt a unique hereditary hand, and while the parents provide the cards, they are not the dealers.

Guilt feelings often motivate parents to embark upon extended searches to determine the cause of their child's retardation. Searches can be well-motivated exercises into understanding the cause of a particular case of retardation and the causes of retardation generally. Quite frequently, however, they are searches for relief from guilt feelings. Some parents feel that if the cause of the child's retardation could be found, it would free them from feelings of responsibility. It would relieve their fear of having contributed to the disorder. This search for a cause can also take place in the context of mutual accusations between the mother and the father about who was "responsible" for the child's condition. Accusations and counter-accusations do not have any basis in fact, but merely reflect the tensions and conflicts already in the family.

It must also be remembered that, even if a particular type of mental retardation has been associated with a chromosome defect, the origin of such a defect is impossible to determine. In one sense, then, the search is fruitless. For even though some physical cause of the retardation may be identified, the question moves back one step—why did this "cause" occur? Therefore, when asking about the cause of a child's retardation, parents should try to determine whether or not they are seeking information to be used in a practical way, such as determining whether genetic counseling will be important, or whether the search is an attempt to reduce their guilt feelings or to assess "blame."

Guilt arising from reactions
to the child

The emotional response that occurs when parents first learn about the condition of their child is profound. So profound, in fact, that it may release a host of responses, many of them primitive and unreasoned. Some of the thoughts and feelings are contradictory; reaction follows reaction in kaleidoscopic fashion. These initial responses, thoughts, feelings, and emotions are to be expected; they are natural events. In part, they are a result of being temporarily overwhelmed by the news. In part, they are a defense against being overwhelmed.

After a period of time it is natural to look back upon this period of maximum stress to ask, "Why did I feel that way?" Some of the thoughts or actions occurring before are now considered unworthy.

At the time of the initial alarm response, the parents' primary goal is to reduce the anxiety in any way possible. The person strives to prevent himself from being inundated by anxiety feelings. Part of this first reaction was what amounts to the rapid testing of ideas, thoughts, and feelings. Because of the urgency of the reaction, this examination of all possible reactions, good, bad, and indifferent, was beyond normal control. But at a later date parents may feel that even momentary thoughts of regret were intolerable.

The fact is that under severe stress the mind tries to consider every possibility as an expression of the body's struggle to maintain itself. This is no more to be governed than an allergic response to ragweed in hay-fever sufferers or the fever that is created by the body when it becomes infected. It is just as unreasoned and inevitable.

Guilt arising from the decision made concerning the placement of the child is a more difficult proposition. There are several ways in which parents can feel guilty. They can feel guilty about not doing the best possible thing for the retarded child or for not doing what will be best for themselves or the other children. They may feel guilty about letting financial, family, or social factors "unduly" influence the decision. They may feel guilty about having had to make a decision in the face of insufficient information. No matter what decision was made and no matter on what basis it was made, there will be uncertainty about the other people and issues involved. These uncertainties are hard to live with, and yet there is no decision or solution which will be entirely satisfactory. Perhaps the only thing that can be done is to admit that no solution will be perfect. Any solution will be a compromise, hopefully the best one possible at the time. It is also important to keep in mind that decisions can be reevaluated and changed. Parents must recognize that the "best decision" at one moment in time may not be the best at another. Values, circumstances, family situation, and the child will change. Decisions must be in tune with the situation as it is, not as it was.

Sadness
While some of the reasons why parents may feel guilty about the birth of a retarded child have been discussed, the sadness often experienced by parents has not. Certainly, feelings of guilt can lead to feelings of exhaustion, despondency, and sadness.

Why should a parent feel sad about a retarded child? In most cases the child will not be in pain or distress any more than any other child. Many retarded children and adults are happy people with even temperaments and friendly dispositions. To state the extreme position, one might argue that they will frequently be happier than normal children born into the same circumstances. Therefore, parents do not feel sad because the child is doomed to unhappiness or to a continuing life of pain or grief. They feel sad for other reasons.

Perhaps this has to do with the fact that the parents can anticipate the limited potential of the retarded child. It is only with intelligence that the effects of the mental limitation in the far-off future can be anticipated. Parents anticipate the future, and this anticipation may be the basis of their sadness.

The retarded child will have a very limited set of choices among which he can make selections. For the normal child, there are unlimited opportunities. For the retarded child, parents know decisions about career goals, a marriage partner, where and how he lives, as well as the enjoyment of abstract and intellectual beauties will be forever restricted. Retarded children are often happy, but happy within limited circumstances. Furthermore, parents recognize that the child's condition is not temporary, that the responsibility for making all important decisions about the child will be up to others, not for a year, not for five years, but forever. This long-term responsibility for decisions probably is another factor that produces sadness and depression. With normal children, parents look forward to a progressive decrease in their own supervision related to the increasing independence of the children. With a retarded child this progression will occur only to a limited degree. Never will the complete responsibility for his or her actions pass to the child.

THREE

RECOVERY
AND
GROWTH

What happens after the first decisions about a retarded child have been made? Whatever was decided, the initial steps have been taken. The mother and father have erected defense systems that are working more or less well. It is at this point that new ways of life may be undertaken to avoid psychological exhaustion. Now the parents must consider themselves. They will have to change in many ways because of their retarded child. As long as they must change, they might as well change in directions which will benefit themselves and the child. They act to refresh their spirits, which may have been reduced to a dangerously low level during the first stress. What are the beginnings of change?

Recognizing the facts
The first thing that must be done is for both husband and wife to admit that they have a child with different and limited capabilities. This should be communicated between husband and wife, as well as to

the people around them. While there is no particular need to broadcast the fact that a child of theirs is retarded (since this might be interpreted as soliciting sympathy and pity), it is important to acknowledge the nature of the child's disorder to people who ask. It is only by talking to others that parents can fully admit to themselves that they have a retarded child.

Parenthetically, it should be noted that when parents tell someone their child is retarded, almost always the response will be annoying in some way. Sometimes the parents will be annoyed by an exaggerated and probably insincere statement of sympathy and concern. Other times the reply will be abrupt and can be interpreted as reflecting a total lack of concern or interest. It is easy at this stage for parents to be offended by almost any remark a person makes. "Oh, but she is such a cute baby." "Why, he looks so normal, I am sure that he must have been misdiagnosed." Remarks such as these will be heard often. They may evoke hostile feelings in the parents, even though the person making such a response is a friend. Consider that the friend is often caught off guard and feels awkward. He wants to ease the problems of the parents by making an appropriate response, but very few people think about the remarks they should make ahead of time. Indeed, what kind of remark could help? There may not be any sensible remark to be made. The parents of a retarded child are in particularly sensitive circumstances, and they must be charitable toward their friends. Remarks should be accepted in the spirit in which they were intended.

Even though the parents have come to admit to themselves and others that they have a retarded child, their feelings about the child and about their situation must be examined. Just as it is a mistake to hide the fact of a child's retardation, so it is a mistake not to try to determine one's deepest feelings about it. The parents must share their own feelings with each other. The benefits of disclosing feelings are twofold: first, clarifying feelings will help establish a meaningful basis for future discussions, which, in turn, will improve future communication. Second, it will lead to a release of emotions and feelings about the baby and each other. *The birth of a retarded child should stimulate the parents' personal growth.* One critical thing is to prevent either the mother or the father from becoming "frozen" by the arrival of the retarded child. *Retirement to a silent inner world is a fatal error.* It is possible for both parents to grow toward greater mutual understanding, which will not only enable them to deal effectively with the present crisis but also will help them to be prepared for unknown problems of the future.

How can disclosure of a husband to a wife and a wife to a husband be facilitated? This is often difficult under the best of circumstances and may become even more difficult with the birth of the retarded child. The first task is for both partners to recognize their need to tell each other their feelings about the retarded child. They must also explore their feelings toward each other. Perhaps the best advice is for each parent to practice disclosing some things with the understanding that there will be reciprocal disclosures by the other. It is almost as simple as saying, "If you tell me a little something, then I will tell you a little something." Feelings are most difficult to express when they come close to the core of the person, including their individual responses to the retarded child.

Disclosing facts or feelings about oneself to another person is a difficult, and often a painful, procedure. At times, it may be that a person hopes that the other person will accept him or her despite "unworthy" impulses or feelings. Since revealing oneself is so difficult and potentially dangerous to a relationship, at the first sign of censure or criticism, the person revealing himself or herself may quit. The game has become too threatening. To maintain communication, both parties must be willing to accept what they hear with a positive and understanding attitude.

Touching the other person can help. This may seem strange, considering that a husband and wife are sharing intimacies. But when two people sit down with the intent of being completely honest and revealing important feelings to each other, the situation is not the same as it is in bed or with a casual embrace in the kitchen. A touch on the arm or an affectionate squeeze of the shoulder can reassure the other person that regardless of the feelings which are about to be disclosed, the other person is prepared to listen and to understand.

Through the help of a professional psychologist, psychiatrist, or marriage counselor parents may learn techniques that will help them understand each other. Seeking professional help is not a weakness, and, ideally, parents should be able to admit the need for temporary help. The relationships within a family are complicated and not easily understood, even by the family members themselves. Professional assistance should be sought early and not as a last resort. By then, it may be too late.

A "self-disclosure exercise" has been developed by Professor Sidney M. Jourard of the University of Florida. It is a device to help people to learn to disclose something about themselves to others. A modified version of it (see pages 72-73) may be useful for parents who find it difficult to tell another person about their feelings.

Roles in life

Each person plays a number of roles. These include husband or wife, parent, businessman or woman, colleague, neighbor, informed citizen, member of church or synagogue, and so forth. Many of these roles will be affected when a retarded child enters the family. It will be helpful for parents to look at their roles and to imagine them as they will be in the future.

Roles are what others expect a person to do in a specific situation. In the family setting there are roles to be played by the mother and by the father. Certain behaviors are expected from a boss and other behaviors from a worker. These expectations are useful because they make behavior predictable in most situations.

Both the mother and father must now face a change in some roles. For example, there may have been a number of parties at which presents for the new baby were given. During the course of the preparations, the mother communicated her own expectations and plans. Friends and neighbors came to anticipate the actions of

A self-disclosure exercise

Here is a way for two people
to learn about each other.

At the right is a list of topics
for conversation. Take turns
going first with your partner.
If you are first, tell husband or wife
everything about yourself related to
the first topic. When you have said
all you have to say, it is
your partner's turn to disclose himself
to you on that topic.

You can ask questions
for more information about the topic
under discussion, but one
should feel free to decline.

Do not press the other person to tell
more than he or she feels comfortable
doing. Do not disclose more than
you feel comfortable disclosing.

When you reach a point of embarrassment
or self-conciousness, simply say to
your partner, "I have reached a limit."

Pay attention to the occasions when
you feel most free, and when you are
most tense; you may learn something
of value about yourself.

73

A self-disclosure exercise

1 *Tell your partner about any aches*
  or pains you may have.

2 *Tell your partner about*
  your personal philosophy of life.

3 *Tell your partner those things*
  which give you strength.

4 *Tell your partner your view*
  of how your parents feel about
  the retarded child.

5 *Tell your partner how you feel*
  about crippled or retarded children,
  in general.

6 *Tell your partner*
  about how you felt when you learned
  that your own child was retarded.

7 *Tell your partner how you feel*
  about your own retarded child.

8 *Tell your partner how you feel*
  about him or her.

9 *Tell your partner what you see*
  the future to be for you both.

the new mother or father. Regardless of the initial decisions made about the placement of the child, conditions are not as they had been anticipated. The parents will behave differently than if the child had not been retarded. How will the mother react? Will she be doting, casual, strong, weak, hostile? What modifications will she make in the mother role? What will the father do? How will he react to the fact that the boy will not be president, or like Joe Namath, or perhaps even able to earn his own living? For the most part, friends will want to tune in and act in accord with whatever attitudes the parents are going to adopt. Business associates and fellow workers will want to know. Their behavior will be based on the role that will be assumed by the father.

Perhaps it is as simple as saying that attention should be given to how the mother and father want others to perceive their reactions to the baby and the decisions that have been made. Once new roles have been assumed, it will be more or less easy for other people to adopt a consistent pattern of relating to the parents.

This is not to say that when a person has adopted a role, the role is a "false front" for others. The parents must be themselves, and if they have not found a satisfactory way of living or have not made firm decisions, then this should be made clear to others. Given personal uncertainty and indecision, it would be a mistake for the father to go to the office or the mother to go to the neighbors for coffee striving to give an impression of strength, certainty, and organization. The discrepancy between these false roles and the underlying feelings would be too great to bear for any length of time. It would be far better to try to determine how best to make others aware of the parents' uncertainties without eliciting feelings of pity and sadness. Everyone has his or her particular difficulties to deal with in life. Friends of parents of retarded children want to help, but they have their own problems to face. These friends want the parents to adopt roles in regard to the retarded child, so that they can deal more or less effectively with the parents and give the type of support that seems to be desired.

It is often difficult to stand outside of oneself to look at the roles maintained in regard to others. We seldom stop to examine how we are seen by other people in different situations. Nevertheless, this is a good time for parents to try to do so.

An opportunity for love
Perhaps the best thing that can happen after the birth of a retarded child is that parents and family become more aware of

the importance of love. Many people show their concern and the fact that they can be counted on for emotional support, love, and affection. What better time to nourish these relationships than when they are most needed?

Love should be cultivated between husband and wife. True concern for the feelings of a partner is perhaps the best reflection of love in times of crisis, but it is also important for the husband and wife to see each other as people, not only as an unfortunate mother or father. How can a *person* be encouraged and loved at this time? The husband might ask, "How can my wife be made happier and have more free time?" "How can I help her become what she wants to be?" The wife might ask, "How can I do things that will allow him to accomplish long-term goals that he has been putting off?"

If the family situation was not all that it might have been at the birth of the child, perhaps this is also a time to reexamine the relationship between the parents. Perhaps it is the time to reinvent the relationship. No relationship between two people is ever stagnant. Since people change, the relationship must change. Often, however, the growth of the relationship lags behind the growth of one or the other of the people involved. Perhaps this is the time in which the changes should be recognized and examined so that the relationship can be modified. Perhaps it is a time to look over the family projects— whether they be those of the husband, of the wife, or of the older children—joint projects and separate projects. Has the priority of the projects been changed? Has their meaning been altered? Such questions are never easy to approach, but perhaps they need to be reconsidered.

Life must have joy in it. It may be difficult for parents to imagine that joy can ever return to their lives. But it can and it must. One approach to joy is through nourishing the love relationships that already exist. As mentioned just above, it is critical to give these every opportunity for growth and development.

Most people find the deepest joys of life come from doing things which go beyond immediate personal interests. Activities whose fulfillment benefit others often are the most joyful of all.

Beyond the self

Most parents of retarded children look for ways in which they can reach out to help others while remaining within a general framework of helping children. They look for ways in which they can become active in an organization that works with or for the interests of mentally handicapped children. This is a reasonable approach, but it often fails to work out well in practice. Often parents of retarded children can make their best and most continuing contribution in dealing with children with other kinds of disabilities or in agencies that benefit people economically or politically.

This is not to say that parents should not join with other parents of retarded children to help one another or to work toward improvements in the programs and schools for retarded children. They need to become active at the community level and to work directly with people in need of assistance of one kind or another. If this is restricted to working with retarded children and/or their families, however, the effort to separate their own problems from those of others will be very difficult. Part of the value in becoming involved in activities beyond those of the immediate family is to introduce a change in the parents' lives. They should not dwell exclusively on their own problems. There are certain practical difficulties in working with groups of retarded children, too. When working with retarded children of other families, parents may find themselves interpreting other children's behavior from what they know about the behavior of their own. This may or may not be helpful to the other children. The parents' own family conditions have provided a basis for reacting to one specific retarded child, but they are almost incapable of making objective judgments about retarded children in general. Working as a volunteer in a private school for retarded children, a parent may react emotionally, and sometimes antagonistically, to the goals set up by the professional educator in charge of the program. It is very difficult for people to realize that they have become less than objective about plans or programs. However, the professional in charge, because of a greater objectivity and more specialized training than most volunteers, does not become so emotionally involved. Working for the best interest of the education of retarded children requires training, objectivity, and experience.

Perhaps a parent's interest in helping children would be better applied to work with culturally deprived children or those suffering from physically crippling disorders. One of the great needs in most cities today is assistance for the underprivileged. For example, clinics of various kinds are being established in the more crowded areas. Transportation and clerical help are constant problems for such clinics. Perhaps a parent of a retarded child could make the most effective contribution in this setting rather than in a school for retarded children.

Programs for the retarded are not greatly advanced by emotion. The most effective way to move the cause of retarded children forward is through the combined political efforts of a group of parents. These groups are usually organized on a local level and must influence officials on the school board and in other state and national bureaucracies.

Organized activities on behalf of retarded children are quite recent. National associations of parents of retarded children have been formed only in the past twenty years in most countries. In general, these parent groups have been of substantial help in improving the conditions of retarded children and adults. These improvements, however, have not been through unreasoned emotional appeals but through a careful and logical analysis of existing conditions and the development of step-by-step programs for the implementation of change. Unreasoned emotional appeals are ineffective and soon forgotten. Most people who are active in political and community life would like to help retarded children and will be happy to do so within their powers. This is true for underprivileged children and for children suffering from various forms of physical abnormalities as well. One of the positive benefits of working in any of these areas is that it is possible to make substantial contributions and to see changes being made. The creation of practical plans depends upon a careful balance of emotion and reason.

A return to the self

Paradoxically, a person only attains fulfillment by going beyond himself to help others. In a sense a person turns toward helping others in order to find himself. A retarded child presents a potent stimulus for a change in life that can be used to further development by helping others in trouble and need. This is reminiscent of one of the remarks of Jesus to the effect that he who would save his life must first lose it to a greater cause. The freedom that is obtained comes from dedication to higher goals and projects, which liberates a person from many of the petty concerns and problems that may have been annoying in the past. It provides access to a host of new ideas, goals, people, and activities that were never dreamed of before. To be sure, there will be some new problems and associated grief. But in working to solve them, fulfillment is found.

One of the signs of personal growth and liberation from the past is a greater awareness of one's individual goals and the extent to which they are being fulfilled. When horizons become broadened, people often find that their initial activities are not what they really wanted. For this reason parents should try several ways of helping others, giving up those that fail to satisfy.

How can one tell if the outside interests are the "right ones"? One way is to see whether or not working in the area produces beneficial effects and satisfaction. These include genuine concern about the people being helped, gratification from the work itself, and an improvement in the parents' overall feelings.

Time

Parents should not expect miracles to happen. The adjustments that follow having a retarded child are difficult and take time. Time itself is a healing influence, provided the parents can achieve a condition in which their own future growth can begin.

Even after the decisions about the child have been made, it will take time for them to be effective in reducing anxiety. Parents will be worried about the wisdom of their decision. They question their own motives. They wonder if they really did take all factors into account. These doubts produce further stress and anxiety. They can be anticipated and arrangements made for evaluating the decisions periodically. The preliminary steps toward reflecting on roles in life, toward helping loved ones, toward new goals will all help, but time is required to evaluate which are successful and which are not. Time will help overcome both uncertainties and anxieties. Relief will not be immediate, but it will come.

Summary and suggestions

Having a retarded child can be a stimulant to personal growth, but growth is more than mere change. Personal growth can be defined as changes in behavior that are in valued directions, changes which make the person better able to cope with life's problems, to enjoy the world, to love and help others. What suggestions can be made that may help in initiating such growth?

1 An examination of goals. Too often people go through life without considering what they want from it. However, a careful examination of behavior often reveals what people value. We indicate our values by the time, money, and attention paid to objects, people, and styles of behavior. If our conscious goals in life differ from those indicated by what we do, this discrepancy should be noted and considered. In essence, this means that parents should ask the questions, "Who am I?" "Who do I want to become?" "How do I feel about myself?"

2 Exposure. Before a person can grow in new, healthful directions, the possibility of such growth must be present. This means that there must be exposure to new avenues for change. The exposure can be direct or indirect. Direct exposure would include first-hand encounters with new people, activities, and ideas. Indirect exposure can come about through reading and from the experiences of others. For the parents of a retarded child, the new exposures must be of two kinds. The first type are those related to mental retardation and to the specific disabilities of the child. This will occur as a result of the "required education" discussed in the next chapter and through contact with parents, educators, and physicians working with retarded people. They will also have direct exposure to the problems of mental retardation through visits to homes, schools, and institutions in which the behavioral effects of retardation can be seen.

The second kind of new exposure is of a more general nature. The parents cannot afford to withdraw into a shell, retreating from the world into armor made from the fabric of defense mechanisms. They must grow as people in their own right, and to do so must have the courage to explore new ideas, find new friends, and develop new interests. They need to be able to consider new, wider perspectives for themselves.

3 Love. The expression of love and affection is one of the great healing influences of life. It will be important for each of the parents to cultivate actively love and affection in themselves, between each other, and among themselves and their children. This implies respecting others as individuals. The love cannot be restrictive and limiting; it must be one that respects the rights of others to freedom and individuality. This is the time to have mutual confidence and trust.

FOUR

REQUIRED
EDUCATION

Having a retarded child can stimulate renewed personal growth of the mother and father. Part of this growth must be educational. Parents and friends of families with retarded children will want to learn more about mental retardation in general and about the conditions leading to the type affecting the particular child. Many excellent books and pamphlets are available. (Some of these are listed in the appendix.) In this chapter a relatively brief explanation of some of the concepts and terms frequently used in connection with mental retardation will be presented.

A retarded child is one thought to be less "intelligent" than a person who is not retarded. But what is intelligence, anyway? Usually we use the word without attempting to define it. It is a word that is used with an implicit understanding that everyone knows what it means. However, when we do think about "intelligence," the notion of a general intellectual ability seems strange, since we know from common experience that some people have much greater musical abilities than others, while others have greater athletic ability. There are a host of abilities and talents which are not equally distributed among people, but is there some general intellectual ability over and beyond the specific abilities that are most often exhibited? The issue may become clearer when "intelligence" is considered more closely.

Intelligence

To go into a theoretical discussion of intelligence or the intricacies of its measurement would be beyond the scope of this book. Nevertheless, certain points should be made. The first is that intelligence is measured by various kinds of tests that are appropriate to people of different ages and with different backgrounds. The scores obtained from these tests predict with some degree of accuracy one characteristic of a person's life: an individual's likelihood of success within the educational system. In one sense, then, "intelligence" refers to a score obtained from one or more tests that tells something about how the individual will progress in school. Given such a limited role for intelligence tests, it is easy to say, "If intelligence test results only tell about success in school, not much stock should be put in them." However, the importance of education is obvious. Many jobs and careers hinge upon educational success. Education is important for understanding and dealing effectively with the world in which we live. Without a modicum of education, many aspects of the world will be completely beyond understanding. People with below-average intelligence test scores tend not to do well in educational programs. People with low intelligence test scores will probably be unable to complete more than a few years of regular school. Individuals with very low test scores probably will be unable to learn to read or write or to complete any regular schoolwork.

Since intelligence test scores are constructed to predict future performance in educational settings, they presumably measure some potential that resides within the individual and which will manifest itself given appropriate conditions. These predictions, oddly enough, are based upon the past study of groups of people and children. The key word is *groups*. Groups of people with different test scores have been followed and evaluated relative to their educational progress, but in these groups not all people with the same test scores do equally well. Within each test score classification some people do better than others. Therefore, it is possible for a person with a relatively low intelligence test score to be successful in advanced education. Intelligence scores say something about how likely this will be, based upon *groups* of people that have been evaluated in the past. At best, they give a rough estimate of the probability of the future performance of an individual. They are guidelines of the broadest sort. In the end each individual is made up of a host of specific abilities that make educational advancement easy or hard.

Intelligence, however, is usually considered to be a property of the individual, something more than a number derived from a particular test. When the term is used in casual conversation, characteristics of intelligent and unintelligent behavior are assumed. Precise definitions of intelligence are difficult to make, but it has been pointed out by many investigators that intelligence cannot be separated from emotional reactivity, attitudes, feelings, moods, and the physical capacities of the individual. In most cases mental retardation is associated with arrested intellectual development and an arrest of other physical or physiological systems of the body. These produce differences in feelings, moods, and so forth, as well as in intelligence. The end result, however, is a person who is handicapped in coping with the problems of everyday life.

Definitions of mental retardation

Today many people tend to define mental retardation in terms of the scores from one or more intelligence tests. Probably the most widely used is the Wechsler Intelligence Scale for Children (WISC). This test produces a score which is called an intelligence quotient (IQ). Traditionally, an intelligence quotient has been thought of as a score that is found by taking the mental age (derived from tests) of the subject, dividing it by his chronological age, and then multiplying the result by 100. The score that gives the mental age of the child sometimes has been defined as the number of accomplishments that a child has in relation to the accomplishments of younger and older children. For example, a given child might be able to do most of the things an average eight-year-old can do. If this child were only six years old, then the IQ would be calculated by dividing 8 by 6. The mathematical division would then produce a result of 1.33. Multiplying by 100 produces an IQ score of 133. If, however, the child with the eight-year-old abilities was 10 years old, then the result would be 8 divided by 10, or .80. Multiplying this by 100 would give an IQ score of 80. According to this approach, a child's abilities are measured relative to those of other children of the same and different ages.

*Wechsler's Intelligence Classifications**

IQ limits	Percent	Classification
130 and over	2.2	Very superior
120–129	6.7	Superior
110–119	16.1	Bright-normal
90–109	50.0	Average
80–89	16.1	Dull-normal
70–79	6.7	Borderline
69 and below	2.2	Defective

*Adapted from D. Wechsler, *The Wechsler Intelligence Scale for Children*, p. 16. Reproduced by permission. Copyright 1949 by The Psychological Corporation, New York, N.Y. All rights reserved. D. Wechsler, *The Wechsler Adult Intelligence Scale*, p. 20. Reproduced by permission. Copyright , ©, 1955 by The Psychological Corporation, New York, N.Y. All rights reserved.

The Wechsler test for children generates an IQ score by a somewhat different approach. However, an IQ score does indicate the relative weakness or strength of the child relative to a group of others of the same age. Given the scores derived from the WISC when administered to a large group, the number of people having IQ scores falling within certain ranges can be determined. Labels can be assigned to these classifications on the basis of the number of people falling within specific ranges. The distribution of intelligence in the population, as reported by Wechsler, is shown in the table above.

Scores derived from intelligence tests, including the WISC, have been widely used, and to some extent overused, in predicting the abilities of people for educational and other purposes. For example, in the past an IQ score of 70 has frequently been used as a line between mental retardation and normality. People with IQs below 70 were considered to be retarded, while those with IQs above 70 were not. Today a test score of 85 is the "magic number" separating the normal from the retarded for many purposes. One might reasonably ask whether there is any substantial difference in ability reflected in a score of 71 as opposed to 69, or 84 as opposed to 85. Given the other differences in specific abilities among people and the considerable error factor in measuring intelligence with any test, it is doubtful that any intelligence score will be of significant value as an absolute boundary between one *type* of mental ability and another. Nevertheless, in every state, significance is given to test scores, since they determine the placement of a child in schools and institutions, as well as establishing the child's legal rights.

The use of IQ scores in the field of mental retardation is difficult to understand because there are several systems for dividing people into diagnostic categories. An example is given on page 95. Three

Classification of the retarded
Schematic diagram of three systems based on
intelligence test scores. See text.

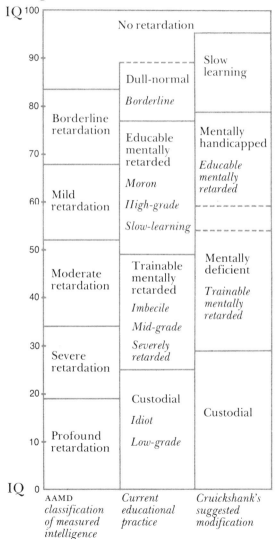

different plans are shown for the use of terms concerning retardation. The top of the scale represents the presumed average intelligence, that is, an IQ of 100. In the left-hand column is the classification system proposed by the American Association for Mental Deficiency (AAMD). In the middle column are terms used on the basis of current educational practices in most areas. On the right-hand side of the figure is the modification of the system proposed by Dr. William Cruickshank. The table on pages 98-99 shows common developmental characteristics of the retarded, using the AAMD system.

The American Association of Mental Deficiency proposed five categories of retardation ranging from borderline to profound on the basis of IQ scores as shown. The present system, which is commonly used in educational systems and which is probably of most importance to parents, starts with a "dull-normal" or "borderline" group whose IQs range from 75 to somewhere below 90. The category *Educable Mentally Retarded* (EMR) includes people with IQs from 50 to 75. The category *Trainable Mentally Retarded* (TMR) is used for people whose IQs range from 25 to 48. Below this are individuals with such limited intelligence that there are not many alternatives to institutional custody.

In general, "educable mentally retarded" has replaced the term "moron," and "trainable mentally retarded" has replaced the term "imbecile." When these terms were first used, they did not have the unfortunate connotations that they have today.

Cruickshank's modification of the system was intended to do two things: first of all, to replace the term "educable mentally retarded" with "mentally handicapped" and "trainable mentally retarded" with "mentally deficient." It is unfortunate that Cruickshank's proposal has not been more widely adopted, since the other terms, "educable" and "trainable," suggest that those within the "trainable range" cannot profit from education programs. This is *not* the case. Many children in the trainable range can learn to read simple materials and to do many things that are compatible with their specific abilities. All children can profit from an educational program that is suited to their specific abilities. For this reason, the terms suggested by Cruickshank should be more widely used.

In addition, Cruickshank proposes the term *slow learner*. He suggests that it be applied to children whose IQ scores fall between 80 and 100. This category was meant to include children with abilities

Developmental Characteristics
of the Mentally Retarded

Degrees of Mental Retardation	Preschool Age 0-5 Maturation and Development
MILD 52–67	Can develop social and communication skills; minimal retardation in sensorimotor areas; often not distinguished from normal until later age.
MODERATE 36–51	Can talk or learn to communicate; poor social awareness; fair motor development; profits from training in self-help; can be managed with moderate supervision.
SEVERE 20–35	Poor motor development; speech is minimal; generally unable to profit from training in self-help; little or no communication skills.
PROFOUND *less than* 20	Gross retardation; minimal capacity for functioning in sensorimotor areas; needs nursing care.

	School Age 6-20 Training and Education	Adult 21 and Over Social and Vocational Adequacy
mild	Can learn academic skills up to approximately sixth grade level by late teens. Can be guided toward social conformity. "Educable."	Can usually achieve social and vocational skills adequate to minimum self-support but may need guidance and assistance when under unusual social or economic stress.
moderate	Can profit from training in social and occupational skills; unlikely to progress beyond second grade level in academic subjects; may learn to travel alone in familiar places.	May achieve self-maintenance in unskilled or semi-skilled work under sheltered conditions; needs supervision and guidance when under mild social or economic stress.
severe	Can talk or learn to communicate; can be trained in elemental health habits; profits from systematic habit training.	May contribute partially to self-maintenance under complete supervision; can develop self-protection skills to a minimal useful level in controlled environment.
profound	Some motor development present; may respond to minimal or limited training in self-help.	Some motor and speech development; may achieve very limited self-care; needs nursing care.

slightly below the average. (It should be remembered that IQ scores are established in such a way that half of the population has an IQ above 100 and half has an IQ below 100.) "Slow learner" would designate those people just below the population average in intelligence. Some of these will have a difficult time in going on to advanced educational programs, and the term probably is an accurate description of the situation in regard to some children. However, the value of the "slow learner" category is debatable, since the addition of a category suggesting diminished mental abilities can lead to its slanderous application.

One unfortunate aspect of labels applied to people with less than average intelligence is that programs and classes tend to be established for, and limited to, people described by the labels. Certainly the mentally retarded need to have specialized experiences and programs. However, retarded children will have some abilities well within the normal range. This should be taken into consideration, and both educable and trainable children should be mixed in with the regular school population whenever their specific skills allow. A person may be perfectly able to do mathematical problems and yet be completely inept at language skills and at reading. In such a case it would seem to make better sense to provide special educational programs for language and reading and to allow the individual to attend regular classes in arithmetic.

Children from the underprivileged segments of the community often have low IQ scores because they have not had the cultural experiences that help them to score well on the tests. Most intelligence tests rely heavily upon the use of language. The questions on tests must be read and instructions understood before they can be answered. Furthermore, some questions deal with events occurring within our society that are presumed to be known by most people. Actually, these questions are directed toward the middle-class segments of the population. The child raised in the ghetto or a rural poverty area does not have the same background of experiences as a child from middle-class areas. These differential experiences of children within a culture affect the test scores obtained. If you ask a child a question about a leaf falling from a tree, it helps to know what a leaf and a tree are. Children from the shady suburbs are more likely to understand simple facts about grass, trees, and leaves than children from the asphalt playgrounds of the inner city. If tests were constructed with items about things found within the city, the bias would be reversed favoring the ghetto inhabitant. Not only does the actual content of test items make a difference, but there are more subtle effects of early cultural impoverishment. Children learn to see what pictures represent through actual experiences with pictures and objects. If a child is raised without magazines or books, he has great difficulty in understanding even simple diagrams that may appear as part of the test materials.

When the educational environments of children improve, intelligence test scores often increase appreciably as well. Studies of children who have moved from disadvantaged rural areas to better school systems show that within a relatively short period of time, gains of 20 or more IQ points are often registered. Part of this has to do with improvement in the educational programs, but part of it also has to do with moving into contact with people by whom education is more highly valued. In any case, the IQ score is not a permanent characteristic of the individual. It depends upon the conditions of testing and the cultural bias of the testing instrument. Improvements in the environment can produce remarkable increases in performance of the child on the tests.

Early testing of intelligence

The identification of mental deficiency or retardation in older children is made on the basis of standardized intelligence tests. Some parents will be concerned with the prediction of academic performance at earlier ages. Unfortunately, there are no recognized tests which can predict academic achievement before the child has reached three years of age. Even at that time, the predictive value of any test is quite limited. How, then, is mental deficiency evaluated early in life?

The answer lies simply in the fact that mental retardation represents a disruption of the developmental processes, both physical and mental. With certain kinds of genetic or metabolic disorders quite accurate predictions of mental ability can be made. For example, if a child is a mongoloid, he or she will have a very limited range of potential later in life. The average IQ of mongoloids is between 35 and 45. Once again, this is an average based upon a large group of individuals. Some individuals will have higher IQ scores and some lower, but the vast majority of mongoloids will have scores close to 40. Similarly, phenylketonuria and other metabolic disorders are associated with a very limited range of intellectual achievement. But what about retardation from other, less obvious causes? How can it be diagnosed?

Physicians watch the growth of a child carefully, even if there are no obvious symptoms of aberrant development. The sequence of development is closely noted, as is the growth of specific parts of the body. For example, a lag in the growth of the size of the head may indicate a developmental disorder that may affect the intellectual development of the child. At early ages this might be the only sign of possible retardation. The point is that before the age of three years, the diagnosis of retardation probably is based upon the child's physiological and physical development, and not upon psychological characteristics. The obvious signs of future problems are those physiological characteristics that are more or less closely associated with profound conditions of mental retardation. One of the physiological abnormalities frequently associated with mental retardation is epilepsy.

Epilepsy

There are many types of epileptic seizures. In all of them there is an abrupt disruption of mental activities. A seizure may be simply a momentary lapse in mental awareness, or it may involve recurrent twitches and spasms of many of the body's muscle systems. It may or may not be associated with observable changes in the appearance or movements of the person. Convulsions, great or small, are classified as seizures because all types are associated with an interruption of cognitive functions during the course of the attack and are believed to be based upon rather similar changes in the activity of the nerve cells of the brain. Some seizures are minor in appearance, revealing themselves only by episodes during which the person seems to have lost touch with the world around him. Sometimes people engage in a set of bizarre actions that are inappropriate to the situation during seizures. They are unaware of these actions.

Convulsions involving the entire body are called *grand mal seizures*. The lapses of attention characterizing the minor epileptic seizures are called *petit mal* seizures. Despite the differences between them, both grand mal and petit mal seizures are forms of epilepsy.

Epilepsy of one kind or another is found in a significant portion of the population. Estimates range from 0.5 to 1.0 percent. This figure does not include convulsions in children that are related to fever or to childhood diseases. The occurrence of a single seizure in childhood does not mean that a child is epileptic. Most children who have seizures during the first year of life never have another one. Naturally, any seizure should be investigated by a physician, but usually a single seizure is not a sign of a permanent epileptic condition.

Some forms of epilepsy have a genetic base. Convulsive disorders tend to cluster in families, but the nature of the inheritance is not well known. It is possible that a tendency for an epileptic condition is inherited but that the tendency is not expressed unless there is damage to the nervous system.

Epilepsy can develop after physical brain damage, diseases, tumors, and from unknown causes. Seizures can begin months and even years after the damage to the brain has occurred. The significance of epilepsy for mental retardation is that a large proportion of children with severe mental retardation also have seizures. In general, the greater the number of disturbances of development, the greater the likelihood that seizures will occur.

The EEG (electroencephalogram), a written record of the electrical rhythms of the brain, is used to help determine the presence of epilepsy. It is obtained by attaching small electrodes (usually silver discs) to the scalp of the individual for several minutes. These electrodes pick up the tiny electrical signals generated in the brain, which are then amplified by electronic devices and written on paper. The entire process is painless. In many ways, the arrangement is similar to the recording of electrical potentials of the heart when obtaining an electrocardiogram (EKG). The signals detected from the brain are much more complex than those obtained from the heart, however. The neurologist examines the brain waves, looking for signs of abnormal electrical rhythms generated by the brain to help him determine whether an individual has an epileptic condition. Information from the EEG may allow him to pinpoint the location of the disturbance or help him decide what further tests need to be done.

People with epilepsy have been greatly helped by the development of new drugs. Quite often a person can be placed on medications that reduce the frequency of seizures or eliminate them completely. Unfortunately, in some cases no drugs seem to help. Because many forms of epilepsy respond well to drugs, the disease is less feared than it was only a few years ago. It is important to find out the condition producing the seizures through competent neurological examinations, since they may be signs of a tumor or other progressive diseases that should be treated before they become too far advanced.

The cerebral palsies
The term *cerebral palsies* refers to a number of disorders of those parts of the brain that control the movements of the body. They can arise from a large number

of causes which affect the development of the child before, during, or after birth. The palsies can express themselves in many ways, and any particular form of disturbance in motor activities can be caused by several different types of developmental abnormalities. Furthermore, the same disorder of the brain can manifest itself in different ways in different people. The cerebral palsies are sometimes associated with mental retardation and with epilepsy.

Spasticity is a term used to describe several forms of motor disorders. It refers to abnormalities of the brain and central nervous system that produce changes in the legs and arms as well as other muscle systems of the body, due to maintained contractions in certain muscle systems. There can be different degrees of spasticity. Sometimes only the legs are involved, but often all limbs and joints are affected. Movements tend to be jerky and spasmodic, combined with a general weakness in the affected muscles.

There are a large number of motor abnormalities that go by names that have specific meanings only to the neurologist. Unfortunately, they will be of little value to most parents. Their value lies solely in their possible contribution to the diagnosis of the disease process by the medical specialists. Parents are most interested in the treatments that can be undertaken and the prospects for the further development of the child.

In many forms of cerebral palsy, only treatments that relieve the most distressing symptoms can be offered. Sometimes this involves brain surgery. However, with the ever-increasing knowledge of the chemistry of the brain, there is hope for the future.

One of the most difficult things about the cerebral palsies is that in some people the motor system abnormalities become less as the child becomes older, while in others the symptoms become worse. An accurate estimate of the future is often difficult even for the medical specialist.

Kernicterus

The term *kernicterus* describes a condition in which certain parts of the brain become damaged late in prenatal development or just after birth. Kernicterus stems from an incompatibility between the blood of the baby and the blood of the mother. Within a day or so after birth, the child begins to show a jaundiced condition (a yellowish appearance) due to the effect of an increase in amount of bilirubin resulting from the blood incompatibility. This excess of bilirubin is thought to have a toxic effect on cells in certain parts of the brain, although other consequences of the blood incompatibility also affect the developing baby.

Each person has many specific chemical "qualities" or "factors" in his red blood cells. These specific factors are complex protein molecules, and they represent one of the ways in which the body recognizes its own substances and distinguishes foreign "invaders." If an invader is found, antibodies are formed to attack and destroy it. For each system of the body there are many sets of "factors" which can be used to identify foreign invaders. The production of antibodies to foreign proteins of the red blood cells takes a rather long period of time to develop. How many specific factors are associated with the red blood cells of the body are not known, but there are many. One of them is called the *Rh factor*. (This term is an abbreviation of the word "rhesus" because it was first identified in the blood of rhesus monkeys.) There are people who are Rh-positive and other people who are Rh-negative. Trouble arises when the baby has an Rh positive blood type and the mother has an Rh negative type. Because the formation of antibodies takes so much time, the first baby of a mother under these conditions often escapes any damage, but during additional pregnancies the mother develops more and more antibodies to the

Rh-positive blood cells. During the second and third pregnancies, these antibodies formed in the mother's body begin to attack the Rh-positive blood of the developing infant.

If a baby is born who soon develops a jaundiced appearance, the Rh factors of the mother and offspring are checked immediately. If there is an Rh incompatibility and other signs of kernicterus, all the blood of the baby is immediately changed by transfusions to a Rh-negative type. If the exchange transfusion of blood is carried out quickly after diagnosis, the outlook for the child is very good. If not, the prospects for future normal development are poor.

A jaundiced condition is not uncommon in a baby in the first day or so after birth. Slightly yellow skin color is relatively common. This "newborn jaundice" stems from entirely different causes than from those producing kernicterus and will clear up by itself within a short period of time. The child suffering from kernicterus develops the jaundiced condition between the first and fourth days of life, and at the same time, there may be other signs of neurological damage. An Rh incompatibility can always be demonstrated through analysis of the blood of the infant and the mother.

Hydrocephaly

Hydrocephaly is a condition in which the head is enlarged, often to a very great extent, by the progressive buildup of cerebrospinal fluid in the brain. It may start as an abnormal condition before birth, or it may begin within the first few days, weeks, or months of life. As with many disorders of the nervous system, it can arise from a number of causes before or at the time of birth. The degree of enlargement of the brain and head may be large or small. Where there is only a mild degree of hydrocephaly, at first few behavioral symptoms may be seen. Where there is a great accumulation of fluids and a great increase in brain size, a host of neurological signs may be seen. These include disorders of the sensory systems, including the eyes, and very severe disorders of motor behavior. The mental abilities of a child suffering from hydrocephaly are hard to predict except in the most extreme cases. Sometimes even a child with a fairly severe case of hydrocephaly may actually show quite a reasonable intellectual development.

At the present time there are conflicting opinions about the treatment of hydrocephaly. Often, however, improvements of the affected child's condition have been shown following the physical implantation of a shunt or valve to reduce the pressure of the cerebrospinal fluid. The most competent neurological and neurosurgical skills should be sought and utilized as soon as the condition is detected.

Microcephaly

This is a vague term used to describe a head below average in size; it is associated with many types of developmental disorders. Small heads are found in people with Down's syndrome and those with phenylketonuria, for example. Substantial reductions in the size of the head and brain can result, however, from imperfect brain development with many different causes. Furthermore, not only can heads be small, but they can be abnormal in shape as well. Growth abnormalities can be represented by changes in the length, width, or height of the skull. Some extreme forms of microcephaly have been found to represent the inheritance of an abnormal condition on a single gene.

The measurement of head size during development is important, since it can lead to detection of conditions related to hydrocephaly or microcephaly. Most physicians measure head size as part of their regular physical examination, although others merely judge it less exactly. In any case, the size of the head is one of the indices of development which should be closely observed.

Inborn errors of metabolism

To grow and to function properly, the brain has to receive an adequate supply of many different materials for its metabolic activities. Some people are born without the ability to form certain enzymes necessary for making the needed supplies or for eliminating them when there is a surplus. In other cases abnormal enzyme and metabolic products are formed. In infancy and childhood the rapidly growing brain is particularly vulnerable to innate metabolic errors.

There are a vast number of inborn metabolic errors. Over 50 types of such errors have been described, and more are being discovered and described every day. Some of the more common innate metabolic errors are phenylketonuria, galactosemia, and maple syrup urine disease. Most of these diseases result in more or less obvious changes in bodily structure and physiological activities. Some inborn errors of metabolism are almost always associated with mental retardation, while others only rarely are. For unknown reasons, the degree of mental retardation varies widely within each of the metabolic disorders. Putting an affected child on a special diet early in life often can greatly reduce the mental retardation frequently associated with some of the diseases. In all cases of metabolic imbalance prompt and competent medical treatment is absolutely essential.

Genetic counseling

Most inborn errors of metabolism and many forms of retardation are inherited in accordance with simple and predictable genetic rules. Where a genetic component of the retarded condition is well known, the probabilities of future children being affected can be calculated. These probabilities may be of vital importance, since they can help parents decide whether or not to have other children. Some of the genetic disorders leading to retardation are inherited in accordance with very complicated, rather than simple, rules of genetics. Furthermore, the probabilities of a retarded child being born change with the parents' age. Therefore, there are no simple rules that can be presented to indicate the likelihood of births of future affected children which can be applied "across the board" to every family with a retarded child. Professional advice must be obtained from a trained genetic counselor.

Genetic counseling is not only useful in making decisions about future children, but it can provide information to the immediate relatives of the affected child.

For example, if a child with Down's syndrome is born as a second child in a family, a genetic analysis can reveal whether one of the parents or the unaffected sibling has the defective gene, too. It is possible for an apparently normal person to be a "carrier" of the syndrome. If the carrier condition is found in a parent or sibling, the odds of their having a child with Down's syndrome are much greater than if it is not found.

Using recently developed techniques, it is sometimes possible to determine whether a child is suffering from disorders leading to retardation well before birth. These techniques are available to prospective parents in many modern medical centers around the country. A list of genetic counseling centers can be obtained from the National Foundation, March of Dimes, 1275 Mamaroneck Avenue, White Plains, NY 10605.

Behavior modification
A term frequently used in connection with children suffering from mental retardation is *behavior modification*. This refers to a technique used to change specific behaviors of adults or children which follows the principles of behavior proposed by Professor B. F. Skinner of Harvard University. In this approach behavior is altered by the application of what are called *rein-*

forcements or *reinforcers* just after the to-be-altered response has occurred. What are these principles, and how should the accomplishments of behavior modification be viewed?

Skinner advocates the rejection of complicated and involved theories of behavior in favor of the intensive study of changes in an individual's behavior upon the application of reinforcements. A reinforcement is defined as a stimulus or an event that changes an individual's behavior. A pat on the back or a message of congratulations may act as a reinforcer. When we give a child a piece of candy or a toy after he does something we want him to, these can be called reinforcers. From this point of view, educators and others interested in changing behavior must find circumstances and procedures that act as reinforcers if they wish to change behavior.

Another aspect of the behavior modification approach is the intensive study of the individual. This means that the circumstances and conditions under which a particular behavior occurs must be carefully studied. Once the behaviors occurring in a situation are understood, then it is possible to attempt a new program of applying reinforcers so that the behavior becomes modified. For example, a child may shout periodically in the home. The behavior modification approach would be to look carefully at the circumstances and occasions of the yells and to look at the responses elicited from parents or others in the child's immediate environment after each yell. Perhaps screaming occurs every time the mother seems to be ignoring the child. The screaming might terminate when the mother comes in and picks up the child. It is important to know both the stimuli in the environment that come before the particular behavior and the effects produced by the behavior. In our example screaming was reinforced by being picked up and held.

The importance of careful, exact, and precise counting of behaviors cannot be overemphasized. The rate of occurrence of a particular behavior and the times at which it occurs must be studied in great detail. Furthermore, as attempts at modification begin, changes in the response rate must be recorded. If there is no change in the rate of the response, it must be concluded that the presumed reinforcer is not effective and a new one must be found.

The use of behavior modification techniques requires a great deal of careful study and experience. It is not something that can be simply undertaken. Specific courses and training programs are necessary in order to become competent in the procedures.

In general, there has been some success reported from the application of the principles of behavior modification to specific behaviors of retarded children. These principles include the enhancement of desirable behaviors and the elimination of unwanted acts. Examples of these unwanted behaviors cover a wide range of activities: not eating certain foods, not sitting at the table during dinner, screaming, crying, bedwetting, and so on. As long as the behavior is specific enough to be counted and observed, it is potentially changeable in its frequency through the appropriate application of reinforcements. Many schools and preschool programs are now modifying behavior through this technique. Some schools are applying behavior modification techniques to the classroom even with advanced courses in mathematics, psychology, science, and history. In principle there is no limit to the range of behaviors that can be changed through behavior modification procedures. Often these procedures work exceptionally well with retarded children. Tantrums, spells of crying, shouting, and other disruptive behaviors in the home and school can be controlled. This makes the situation around the retarded child much more livable and acceptable to the family, teachers, and schoolmates.

Most of the better programs for retarded children that use behavior modification principles in a school setting also have developed instructional programs for the parents. It would be a great waste if the child successfully learned to control his crying and shouting at school but not at home. To be maximally useful, the home and school programs must be coordinated. Parents must come to understand the principles of behavior modification and how to apply them to specific behaviors. This is part of the educational program that they must face to become better equipped to deal with any behavior problems that might arise with their child.

Behavior modification is not a panacea for all behavioral problems. There is no doubt that it is an effective procedure for altering some specific behaviors. Nevertheless, most parents discover that their major concerns are *not* specific behaviors but rather a whole range of problems. Behavior modification is only applied to one particular behavior through one particular reinforcement program. To be sure, once one behavioral act comes under control, then it is possible to move on to change another. But gaining control of a single unwanted behavior requires time. The application of behavior modification techniques requires a consistent and deliberate approach to the child in which the appropriate reinforcement is applied uniformly after each and every response. The lowering of the rate of this undesirable response may take weeks or even longer. Nevertheless, it does work given the determination of the parents and teachers to make it work.

Sometimes families actually make use of the disruptive behaviors found in the home. It is a sad thing, but disruptive behaviors of a child can be the glue with which a family is held together. Once the disruptive behavior is reduced or eliminated, other symptoms of the fundamental differences among family members come to light. They may have been hidden in the combined effort to control or alleviate the disruptive influence of the retarded child. When behavior modification is applied, and the disruptive behavior becomes less frequent, other troubles within the family manifest themselves. For this reason, the elimination of a particular disrupting behavior of a retarded child does not always represent a perfect solution to family difficulties. Behavior modification is a beautiful technique for accomplishing its particular purpose: the management of one specific behavior. If other problems exist within the family, due in part at least to the behavior of the retarded child, the parents should also participate in a program to understand their own relationships better.

Patterning

In recent years, a behavioral method for working with normal and abnormal children, called *patterning,* has been described in various publications by Doman and Delacato.* Rather exceptional claims have been made for the success of these techniques, which include the relief of communicative and perceptual disorders and speech and reading disabilities, the enhancement of intelligence, and the improvement of aberrant behaviors. It has been recommended both for intellectually handicapped and normal children.

Patterning is based on a belief that the development of the individual human resembles the evolutionary development of man. Children who deviate from the normal course of individual and evolutionary development can be readjusted to it by behavioral techniques that put them

*See Delacato, C. H., *The Treatment and Prevention of Reading Problems* (Springfield, Ill.: Charles C Thomas, Publisher, 1959), and *Neurological Organization and Reading* (Springfield, Ill.: Charles C Thomas, Publisher, 1966); Doman, G. and Delacato, C. H., "Train Your Baby To Be a Genius" (*McCall's Magazine,* March 1965).

back into step with the appropriate developmental sequence. The advocates of patterning maintain that this can be done by
physically imposing patterns of movement
and behavior upon the child who does not
exhibit them spontaneously. Patterns of
crawling, creeping, and walking are
forced upon the child by adults trained in
patterning. If the child does not have the
proper pattern of motor development at a
specific stage, then all succeeding levels of
development will be affected. According
to this view, it is important to make sure
that the sequence of movements beginning with flexures of the trunk, crawling
in such a way that the arm and leg on the
side to which the head is turned are simul-
taneously flexed while the opposite limbs
are extended, creeping with alternating
flexed and extended arms on the same
side, crude walking, and more advanced
walking are all performed in an orderly
sequence.

Training in these various developmental stages of motor activity is usually
accomplished through the help of three to
five people who manipulate the arms, legs,
and trunk of the individual for specified
amounts of time each day, seven days a
week, without exception. Once the techniques of manipulation and patterning
have been acquired by the members of a
family, they and their friends undertake

the program of manipulation and training.

It has been very difficult to assess the effects of patterning on the development of retarded children. The published data from which conclusions could be drawn are quite meager. A detailed analysis of the patterning method has been reported in an article published in *Pediatrics* by Cohen, Birch, and Raft.* These authors conclude that there is little if any positive evidence to support the claims made by the advocates of the Doman-Delacato programs. They point out that most of the benefits of patterning have been obtained by using more traditional educational techniques and by simply improving the environment of the child.

The enthusiastic reports from people applying the techniques of patterning almost always describe changes in a single individual over the course of the patterning treatment. It is impossible to determine whether these changes have any relationship to the regime that has been imposed upon the child. The report by

*Cohen, H. J., Birch, J. G., and Raft, L. T., "Some Considerations for Evaluating the Doman-Delacato 'Patterning' Method," *Pediatrics* 45 (1970): 302 –14.

Cohen, Birch, and Raft concludes that "the data thus far advanced are insufficient to justify affirmative conclusions about the (patterning) system of treatment. Consideration of the statistics of individual case reports suggest that the changes obtained may reflect normal growth and development occurring independently of the method applied, or the inadvertent consequences of social stimulation and environmental change inherent in, or resulting from, the application of almost any method" (p. 313).

Advocates of patterning have written articles that can be found in popular magazines. These optimistic articles may raise the hopes of parents that substantial degrees of improvement can be obtained through these techniques. Many parents with a retarded child look for almost any avenue or approach that will offer some chance, however slight, of enhancing the limited abilities of their children. The raising of hopes which may not be realized is to be deplored. As stated above, at the present time there is no evidence that the patterning approach can improve the abilities or performances of a child over and beyond that which would be expected on the basis of the normal sequence of development in the home or in a preschool program of a traditional sort.

There is another aspect of the Doman-Delacato program which must be considered. The patterning regime is a demanding one. At least four times a day, a number of adults must passively manipulate the person engaged in the program. This requires a great deal of time and effort on the part of those "helping" the child. Ultimately, the family must turn to friends and neighbors to assist with the regime. The training goes on day after day, week after week. It is not something that can be undertaken lightly. The regime may come to dominate the lives of the parents and their friends. This amount of effort would be well justified, of course, if positive gains could reasonably be expected from the program. Without a reasonable likelihood of success the demands upon family and friends become difficult to justify.

Not only does the training regime of patterning demand a great deal of effort on the part of the family and friends, but it also imposes a considerable amount of stress upon the child. Several times each day adults assemble to passively manipulate the child. Quite often this is a stressful experience. The child may come to resent the treatment program and may struggle and fight to avert the exercises being imposed. The stresses induced by the procedures could lead to the development of emotional problems that will aggravate the family's circumstances and the child's difficulties.

All of this is to say that the undertaking of a treatment program based on the principles of patterning should be undertaken only with the greatest degree of caution and with the full understanding that there are only anecdotal reports of its success. Such reports provide no scientific basis for evaluation of the effectiveness of the procedure. Also, it must be undertaken with the view that the procedures can lead to additional difficulties in the child, as well as to possible benefits. The parent must not be misled by unrealistic hopes. Before undertaking a "patterning" program, it would be wise for parents to talk to other parents of retarded children who have been in a "patterning" program. Usually the pediatrician or the county association for retarded children can provide them with the names of parents who have had experience with such procedures in the past. The parents should ask about the successes and failures experienced by these other parents. They should ask about the demands that will be placed upon them and about the emotional effects of the programming upon the child. The burden, once again, falls directly upon the parents' shoulders. They must do their "homework."

FIVE

PROGRAMS
FOR
THE RETARDED

The purpose of any program designed to assist the retarded should be to help each person realize the fullest development of his or her capacities. These include capacities for work, for play, and for all of the many ways in which any person finds fulfillment. In this chapter we will consider some of the programs designed to assist the mentally retarded progress to the best of their own abilities. How many of these programs are available in any one community depends upon many factors. These include the relative wealth of the county and city, the past successes of local parent groups in pressing for programs, and the efficiency of the state governmental agencies charged with helping retarded citizens. It is up to the parents to discover how many of the needed programs are available for their child, as well as to ascertain the qualities of those that do exist.

The services that should be provided in any community fall in different classifications relative to the child's age and degree of retardation. The programs include those for (1) preschool children; (2) school-age children in the public schools; and (3) post-school-age adults. Effective programs for these three age groups should allow many retarded individuals to remain in society and consequently to reduce the need for institutional care.

The degree of retardation is an important consideration. Children with IQs in the 50–85 range are disadvantaged in educational settings but often can function quite well, and even make exceptional contributions, in nonschool settings. Thus, the nature of the programs designed for people with mild or moderate degrees of retardation will be markedly different from those for people with severe or profound retardation. The severely and profoundly retarded are not only disadvantaged in education but also in handling many of the day-to-day problems of life. The nature and amount of supervision required for a retarded person working in the community are related to his degree of retardation and his special aptitudes.

Society's ideas about retarded children are swinging away from historic attitudes that such children should be hidden from public view by being placed in institutions in remote areas. By being hidden from sight, the children did not trouble the public conscience. The current change in philosophy is reflected in the substantial amounts of federal, state, and local funds being used to provide both facilities and services at the preschool, public-school, and post-school-age levels in the community. The aim of these programs and services is to assist parent and local community agencies to provide opportunities and support for the retarded so that they can remain in the community either permanently or for a much longer period than previously possible.

The goal of keeping retarded individuals out of institutions is founded on the belief that institutions must be "bad places." Like prisons, they are thought to restrict the joys and pleasures of their inmates. Their bleakness is thought to further impair the retarded's already meager potential. Most of the data for this negative view of institutions come from studies conducted twenty and more years ago. They do not reflect the rather remarkable changes that have been produced in institutions in many (but not all) states.

The motives of state and federal governments, however, are not entirely based upon what is best for the retarded individual. They are based upon economics, too. It is cheaper to put money into programs that provide ways for the retarded to remain outside institutions. The yearly cost of institutionalization probably runs to more than six thousand dollars per person. Even with prodigious amounts of support, the community programs will be less expensive. Thus, the relatively large amounts of money now being poured into school and job placement programs represent the vision of an accountant as much as that of a humanitarian. In some states bills have been passed by the legislature that force a planned reduction in the number of people who will be allowed to remain in the state institutions. As the state funds supporting the institutions are decreased, additional funds (but smaller in amount) are made available to support rehabilitation programs, foster homes, and small-group living situations in the community.

Even though each state, community, and county has an opportunity to obtain state and federal funds, the quality and amount of services for the retarded vary considerably between one community and the next. Opportunity is not actuality. Someone must prepare the applications for funds to support programs; someone must administer them; and there must be a continued planning for the future. Several factors are related to whether or not good programs are available in any area.

One factor is related to the energy and activity of local groups with an interest in the affairs of the retarded. The local associations for retarded children have been the driving force behind the establishment of preschool programs and the work-related programs for young retarded adults in many areas. Where active parent groups exist, there are likely to be better programs for the retarded individuals. Another factor is the relative wealth of the city or county. In recent years federal programs to aid the causes of retarded children provided almost full support in the first year or two but then declined over the next several years. For example, in the first year of a program, the federal government might support 75 percent of the total cost of the operation, but in the second year this percentage would be reduced to 50 percent. In the third year federal support might be reduced to 25 percent, and by the fourth year there could be no federal support. Local city and county groups were supposed to add their funds to replace the federal dollars being withdrawn. For the programs to continue, funds from the United Way, donations from local community-oriented groups, individual donations, and funds from local government had to be found. In wealthier counties these funds were more easily obtained than in poor counties.

This declining - amount - of - federal-funds approach to the financing of programs for the retarded is being changed.

More consistent federal support over the years is becoming available. Nevertheless, the quality and extent of the local programs is directly correlated with the willingness or the ability of the cities and counties to provide contributions to programs, even though the majority of the funds come from the federal government.

Even with an active parent group and with a reasonable amount of local financial support, whether it be from charitable or from local tax funds, enlightened administrative leadership is required to provide good programs for the retarded. In areas where talented professional administrative leadership has been found, programs have tended to flourish. Where a mechanism to provide a continuing administrative leadership has not been found, even well-financed programs tend to fail. In some instances this administrative leadership at the local level has come from skilled volunteers who devote years of their lives to the programs for retarded children. Sometimes these are people with independent wealth who can neglect other responsibilities to help meet these specific needs of the retarded in the community. In most instances, however, the creative leadership has come from people paid to devote full-time effort in initiating programs, directing them, and keeping lines of communication open between the local agencies and the federal and state administrative agencies.

The complexities of financial administration of local programs have grown enormously in the past few years. Only a few years ago many programs for the retarded only needed someone to accept money from the United Way and other charitable groups, and to dispense the funds sensibly. Today, separate grant proposals must be written for federal funds for each type of community program on forms that are so complex that they put the long form of the income tax return to shame. Reports on the expenditures of the funds require equal attention to detail. The part-time amateur administrator of community programs for the retarded is no longer sufficient.

Preschool programs

If children remain in a community setting, either in their real homes or in foster homes, by the time they are two or three years old they should be enrolled in a preschool program. These are frequently sponsored and organized by local parent groups, churches, or other civic-minded organizations. Specialized preschool programs for retarded children are necessary, since these children often present special problems. For example, many are not toilet trained by the ages at which children typically enter preschool programs. Some retarded children suffer from convulsions or other physical disabilities in addition to their mental retardation.

Preschool programs must be directed toward meeting the needs of each child. Each requires special training that will allow him to move into special education programs in the public school system. Every child should be evaluated upon entering a preschool program. Furthermore, the parents should be asked to indicate the specific behavioral problems with which they need the most help. Individualized programs should be available to meet the particular deficiencies of each child which make his adjustment to the public school system difficult. Before entering a preschool program, the child should be given a complete physical examination and psychological evaluation by a competent psychometrician. The results of these examinations often reveal characteristics of the child which will be of use to the staff of the preschool program. It is especially important to determine any deficiencies of sight or hearing. In many cases such deficiencies have been confused with mental retardation. At the beginning of a preschool program it is important for the parents and the school personnel to be fully aware of the child's mental and physical condition, as well as his personality characteristics.

Many approaches are used by preschool programs to reach their goals. The specific programs found in any school will reflect the training of the teachers and the director of the program. In many communities, these people are qualified special education teachers, often with master's degrees. In addition to the director of the preschool program and the other teachers and aides involved with it, there should be a group of both parents and educators in the community, operating in a supervisory relationship to the program. No matter how good a director the program may have, guidance and direction must come both from parents and from people who have professional qualifications but are not directly associated with the program. When investigating a possible preschool program, the parents should not hesitate to ask about its administrative structure. Does it have an effective advisory group? How is the composition of this group determined? How often do they meet?

As in all matters, parents must examine the ongoing activities of the preschool program firsthand. Over and above the administrative details and practices which have been discussed above, the school should be a happy place. The children should enjoy themselves and be engaged in useful activities. It should not merely be a custodial facility.

Preschool programs should also provide extensive blocks of time during which the child is out of the home. Whether or not there are other children in the family, a retarded child takes a lot of the parents' time and energy. A preschool program is blessed relief to many parents. It gives the mother time to do the shopping and other necessary chores about town. The released time often results in a greatly improved family morale. If preschool programs did nothing more than to relieve the parents of some of the daily problems of care for the retarded child, they would justify themselves. But they can do much more than this. They can be effective learning and training experiences for the children. They can prepare the child for public school and for later life.

The most effective preschool programs are those in which the school situation is integrated with the life of the family. In such integrated programs the goals pursued in the preschool program are supplemented by training in the home. There should be frequent meetings between the director of the preschool program and the parents to evaluate the progress of the child in reaching established goals.

Preschool programs are usually not

free. However, in most communities the parents' "ability to pay" based on income, the number of dependents, and family expenses, determine the amount of tuition that is charged. Most programs run by local associations for retarded children will never refuse admittance to a child because of an inability to pay. Totally private programs are more expensive, of course. Probably the actual cost per month per retarded child in a preschool program is about $200, but very few families could afford this much. Most of the community-based programs charge up to a maximum amount of $50 per child per month. The actual tuition payments are scaled down from the usual maximum of about $50 per month to $1 or less per month in the case of families at lower economic levels. The remainder of the actual cost is made up from state and federal grants to the sponsoring agencies and by contributions from charitable groups.

Public school programs

The quality and character of special education facilities for retarded children vary considerably between one community and another. Each school board or administrative unit fulfills its duty in regard to special education in a different way. Frequently there are two types of classes offered in special education: those for the educable and those for the trainable mentally retarded child. Programs for the educable groups are usually directed toward the acquisition of simple academic skills, such as reading, writing, and mathematics. The program for the trainable groups is directed toward the acquisition of simple motor and language skills.

In an ideal world, the programs for retarded children would be geared to the individual's capabilities and capacities. All too often this is not possible, due to the large numbers of children assigned to a particular school or classroom. However, school administrators are coming to recognize the need to prepare retarded children for effective lives in the community. Unfortunately, too many existing programs, especially those for the trainable clients, remain custodial in nature and do not try to educate the retarded for the outside world.

When a retarded child enters a public school program, the parents will want to become actively involved with parent-teacher associations and with the groups of parents who are striving to improve the conditions for the retarded. It will be necessary for the parents to visit the classrooms, to talk with the teachers and the school administrators and, if necessary, help organize activities to establish new programs for all retarded children.

In the past it has been common for a school board or the administrative officers to establish arbitrary cut-off points in terms of IQ or physical abilities that eliminated some retarded people from benefiting from the public school programs. Often these discriminated against individuals at trainable levels and perhaps even those in the low educable range. Recently, legislation has been passed in many states which requires educational programs be established for *every* school-age child, regardless of his measured level of mental functioning. These legislative acts have been passed largely because of the strenuous activities of county, state, and national associations for retarded citizens. What they do, in effect, is to require the school boards to accept retarded children of all mental abilities and without regard to physical limitations into suitable educational programs throughout the school ages. The effects of such legislation have not been entirely settled. In many states court action will be required to establish the rights of retarded children to public education.

There are also cases pending in several states throughout the country which argue that a person's mental abilities as revealed by scores from standardized mental tests should not provide the basis for discrimination within a school system. The argument is that the use of intelligence test scores provides an unfair basis for admission to a program and thus represents a denial of the retarded child's basic rights. These law suits are being pursued independently of suits in regard to mandatory school attendance. They follow the general argument that education should not be denied an individual because of race, creed, or tested mental abilities.

While it is impossible to discuss a uniformly acceptable set of criteria for special education programs for the retarded, it is possible to point out certain characteristics which are important for their evaluation. First of all, the students in the educational programs should want to go to school. There is no reason school should be an unhappy experience for any child. To the extent the school does not provide a stimulating program, the children will give the appearance of being inmates of a dull institution. Unannounced visits to the schools can easily enough show the enthusiasm and vigor of the students and the school personnel.

Another characteristic of poor educational programs is inflexibility of educational categories. In such programs it is difficult or impossible for a child to move from a program for those classified as "trainable" into one for those with an "educable" classification. It should also be possible for a child in an "educable" classroom to move into a regular school classroom, at least for certain subjects. Ideally, a school should have a regular program of evaluation for each child relative to his individual goals. His progress should be monitored with an eye to moving him into different programs and classes when possible. At more advanced educational levels, it is desirable to have the retarded students attend regular classes for activities in which they may be skilled, since the retarded individual represents a unique mixture of skills, capacities, and interests. This means that there will be certain areas in which he or she will be indistinguishable from nonretarded students. (At least this will be the case for people with moderate degrees of retardation.) Therefore, programs that allow students to participate in classes for which they are suited, regardless of the classification scheme, should be encouraged. Where there are flexible programs the retarded child comes to recognize that he *can* get along with students in regular classes and that he has his own special areas of competence. At the same time, students in regular classes may come to realize that most students in the special education programs do have important contributions to make. Perhaps most important is that the curricular flexibility should blur the boundaries between those in the "special programs" and those in the regular classes. As will be discussed later in the chapter, the label of "mentally retarded" is one which everyone tries to avoid, including those who are retarded. To be classified as "retarded" is to be considered less than a whole person in our society. People with diminished mental abilities may spend their entire lives trying to overcome this stigma. To the extent to which the branding of a person by classification within a school system can be avoided, it should be.

For the retarded student, the end of his public school experience should have made him ready for a meaningful life in society. He should be able to use public transportation, have skills that provide employment opportunities, and have knowledge of day-to-day living in society. To the extent that these goals have been realized, the public school educational program can be judged as successful.

Certain difficulties arise in many school systems concerning the age at which the educational programs terminate for the retarded. Some states require only that a child must be in school until age 16. Yet many children remain in school until the age of 21 if they have not obtained their high school degrees. Often a retarded child needs to remain in school after he is 16 to acquire those skills necessary for later life. Once again, it will be important for the parents of all the retarded students to work with the school board to establish a reasonable age limit for the program.

Upon completion of a high school program, the services of the local vocational rehabilitation agencies will be useful. Quite often funds are specifically set aside in social service agencies for rehabilitation of the retarded. The sorts of services which can be provided by rehabilitation services include an evaluation of a candidate's work potential and his enrollment in skill training programs. These may, or may not, be associated with the high school programs, depending upon the community involved.

Sheltered workshops: a transition

The vocational programs offered by the public schools and by rehabilitation services try to prepare the retarded adult for successful employment in the community. Yet vocational rehabilitation programs are of limited duration and may not be sufficient to allow students to have independent work careers. A transitional work setting must be available. These are often called "sheltered workshops." These workshops should provide a place in which retarded adults can work under special supervision and guidance to the maximum of their abilities.

These special work settings should not only provide a transition from work-training programs to the anticipated employment conditions within the community, but also help some of the retarded who have forms of intellectual impairment that prevent their employment in the normal business settings. Sheltered workshops should provide employment for the retarded who cannot conform to the usual work conditions. They should offer an effective way to provide gainful employment to those who would otherwise not be working.

When entering a sheltered workshop, the retarded individual should be evaluated for his mental and physical abilities, as well as for his present job skills. He should then be assigned to a type of activity having demands appropriate to his own particular abilities. A job in a sheltered workshop should not be a dead end. Each job should be designed to be suitable for people with certain types of limitations and yet provide opportunities for the improvement of job skills. From time to time, job skills should be reevaluated. The clients in the workshop should be advanced from job to job as their skills improve. Through a graduated series of learning experiences, an individual should come to have abilities and habits that make him employable outside of the sheltered workshop. Some retarded adults learn to be accomplished woodworkers, gardners, repairmen, seamstresses, cook's helpers, and machine operators. Quite often they can do just as well on simple jobs as non-handicapped people. A good program will be designed to increase progressively the individual's skills and talents.

One of the main goals of a sheltered workshop is to make a retarded individual capable of self-guided life in the community. As mentioned, this may become a reality through the serial progression to ever more difficult assignments in the sheltered workshop. However, it sometimes happens that the move from a sheltered workshop into the community fails. Some individuals find that they cannot cope with the normal conditions of employment. Therefore, the sheltered workshop should also provide a place to which the person can return if he or she has not been successful on the outside. In this sense, sheltered workshops can provide a firm base camp to fall back upon for the retarded who are trying to learn to deal with society.

Some retarded people will never be able to get along outside of sheltered workshops. Therefore, a sheltered workshop must also be a place of employment on a more or less permanent basis for those who need it.

Sheltered workshops should provide more than training for employment. They also should provide an opportunity for a social life beyond that of a home, foster-home, or group-living situation. More-over, many sheltered workshops have active programs to further the education of their clients. Sheltered workshops should play important roles in the economic, educational, and social lives of their clients.

One of the major difficulties with most, if not all, sheltered-workshop programs for the retarded is that they tend to cast the stigma of mental incompetence on those who are employed in it. Within a community the workshops are known as places where only the "mentally unfit" work. Every retarded adult wants to escape the stigma of mental incompetence, and yet most sheltered workshops are publicly designated as specifically for the retarded. One answer to this problem is to have sheltered workshops that are not only for the benefit of the mentally retarded, but also for people suffering from many sorts of handicaps. These would include people who are blind or deaf and those with paralytic conditions. Sheltered workshops that offer services to people with several types of disabilities may provide a more useful experience to all concerned than those geared specifically to only one type of disorder. People who suffer from one type of handicap can assist those suffering from another. They can learn about each other's handicaps. In fact, to have people suffering from different types of handicaps within the same work situation actually makes for more efficient production. From the perspective of the mentally retarded, the most important consideration is the fact that the inclusion of people with many different types of handicaps in a sheltered workshop produces a situation in which the mentally retarded escape the onus of working in a place which is *only* for mentally incompetent people. Unfortunately, few communities have sheltered workshops that serve more than one sort of disability. This is certainly a goal to be sought in the future.

The changing roles of institutions

In the past, too many retarded individuals could only look forward to a life within an institution. Years ago many institutions were essentially jails in which the daily life of the retarded individual was restricted and unexciting. With the advent of an awareness that a retarded individual is a real person with certain handicaps but also with certain areas of special skills, the nature of institutions has been changing.

Institutions are seen as offering a variety of services rather than as being a place where the retarded are kept out of society's way. Some of these services are transitional. They can provide education, training, and therapies designed to help individuals move from the institution into foster and group-living homes. In those settings they can take part in community-based programs. Institutions can also act as "home" for residents working in the community.

It must be remembered, however, that with even the most effective of community programs there will still be a substantial demand for care of the retarded in institutions. Institutions will be needed for the profoundly retarded and the retarded with other physical, or even possibly emotional, handicaps which prevent them from independent living. Furthermore, many retarded individuals only slowly come to develop those skills and knowledge which will allow them to take employment and to live with the social and cultural complexities of modern life. Institutions can provide specialized training and educational programs directed toward making all of their residents more independent, whether or not the resident is likely to make his own way in the world.

In many cases it is difficult to determine whether or not an individual will be able to live outside an institution. Institutions should provide a base from which a person can move gradually toward testing his competencies in the community. With the firm base of the institution, the person can find an appropriate degree of independent life. Too often a retarded individual has been thrown into the community without proper preparation and without sufficient training. It is fitting and proper for the institution to maintain constant surveillance of people to help them achieve as much independence as possible.

Therefore, institutions will continue to play important roles in all of the programs directed toward helping individuals with various degrees of retardation. Many will have to be in an institutional setting for many years and some for their entire lives. This does not mean that institutions must have only custodial responsibilities. Many progressive institutions provide warm surroundings in which the residents can have profitable and useful lives, while providing guidance and control proportional to the abilities and needs of their particular residents.

What sort of lives do the retarded live when they move outside institutions? What happens to a retarded individual after he finishes his job-preparation program within the public school system or after a post-school-age vocational rehabilitational program?

The adult in the community

Most of the irrational fears some people have had about releasing the retarded into the community have proved unfounded. Some people feared that the retarded might become social deviants, that they would turn to crime because they would not understand the difference between right and wrong. Most studies have shown that very few retarded individuals living on their own get into any type of difficulty with the law. They tend to live within the context of the society and do not present a law-enforcement problem.

Even though the retarded living outside institutions are law-abiding citizens, this does not mean that their lives are rich or full. Most cannot be considered successful in the ways in which we usually define "success" in our society.

What sorts of problems do retarded adults face when they are outside of the institutional structure? Their problems are exactly those faced by everyone. These include (1) making a living, (2) management of sexual activities, marriage, and children, and (3) the use of leisure time. The solutions to these problems are complicated by the limited intellectual capacities of the retarded individual and sometimes by prior experiences in an institution that have made the retarded person insecure and self-conscious. If a retarded person has lived within a family situation that was overly protective, he may have trouble in situations in which this degree of protection is no longer available. He may find it difficult to make decisions and plans for himself. For some, the relatively simple acts of planning meals or even selecting them from a restaurant menu is difficult. Being mentally retarded does not insulate anyone from other types of troubles. The retarded can suffer from mental and psychological difficulties, which may result from their past training and experiences in addition to their intellectual handicap.

Most of the studies that have been done on retarded individuals living in the community have investigated people whose IQs range from 50 to 85. However, IQ is not a good measure of how well a person will get along in his own society. The ability to cope effectively with the demands of daily living are not directly related to IQ. Some people do reasonably well on their own with an IQ of 60, whereas others with an IQ of 85 cannot seem to make it. Probably this depends upon mental and behavioral characteristics of the individual not measured by IQ tests. As mentioned before, measured intelligence is only one component of mental adjustment.

As might be expected, most of the re-

tarded individuals who live outside of institutions are definitely handicapped in
their employment prospects.* Most positions with significant economic status require advanced educational skills. By defi-
nition, the retarded have their greatest
handicap in the educational area. Most
jobs require at least a high-school education. Many employers look for applicants
with two or more years of college. The
employment opportunities that are open
to the retarded are those at the very lowest
of the socioeconomic scale.

About half of the retarded individuals
living on their own are more or less con-
tinuously employed. Another 25 percent
are employed "most of the time." The positions they fill are menial ones: dish-
washer, field hand, unskilled laborer, jani-
tor, or custodian, all under direct
supervision. Often they find jobs in small
businesses, filling jobs that other people
refuse. Sometimes these undesirable positions are grossly underpaid, while other
positions have working conditions that are
so deplorable that most people are not
willing to accept them. Yet unemployment
is greatly feared by the retarded. They are

*Much of the information in this and the following
paragraphs comes from R. B. Edgerton, *The Cloak
of Competence: Stigma in the lives of the mentally retarded.* Univ. of Calif. Press, 1967.

afraid that if they are unemployed they will be returned to an institution. Perhaps even a stronger consideration is that being employed provides a mechanism of attaining self-esteem.

Even with a great willingness to work, most retarded are marginal wage earners. They are often in debt. They tend to have little job security, since most have few marketable skills. Hopefully, vocational rehabilitation programs and job-oriented public-school programs will provide needed work skills for the retarded, so that they can become eligible for better jobs with greater job security.

If a retarded individual loses a job, it is often difficult for him or her to understand how to go about finding another one commensurate with his skills and past experiences. There must be some mechanism to provide job counseling and guidance to help retarded citizens find new positions.

Related to the low economic status of the employment positions available to the retarded is the fact that most of them live in lamentable conditions. Seldom does a retarded individual own a home or an automobile. The written examinations required for drivers' licenses are a substantial handicap to driving. Many have difficulty in learning how to tell time, to make change, or to understand the value of money. All of these are serious handicaps in day-to-day living. For the most part, those who are employed and participate in the economic life of the community do so because they have found some person to give them guidance and direction in their private and economic lives. In the past, finding such a person was a matter of luck. As more and more retarded come to live in the community, mechanisms for providing this direction must become more formalized and become a matter of routine. Without guidance, the retarded are prevented from living up to their fullest capacities.

At one time it was feared that the retarded would engage in sexual practices which were well beyond the range of the "normal." Data collected concerning the sexual activities of retarded individuals indicate that they are rather conventional and not different from those found in normal individuals living at the same socioeconomic level. Many of the retarded women marry, and most of these tend to stop working when they are married. This is related to the fact that many of them marry normal men who refuse to let their wives work. The men with normal intelligence who marry retarded women tend to want dependent, submissive, and totally appreciative wives. They help their wives in many ways. While many retarded women marry normal men, the reverse is seldom found. The retarded men seldom marry or establish lasting relationships with normal women.

In the area of leisure activities, the retarded living in normal communities tend to be engaged in a relentless pursuit of happiness. They enjoy conversation and television to a great degree. Their use of drugs and alcohol are about the same as found in normal people of the same economic status. On the other hand, very few have any interest in religious or political affairs. Few, if any, of the retarded independently living in communities have ever voted in city, state, or national elections.

The retarded individual is intensely motivated to remain outside the walls of an institution. He is dedicated to maintaining a freedom from the direction and guidance found in most institutions. All want to be accepted as normal people and to avoid the stigma of "mental retardation." All are afraid of being returned to an institution. In institutions they resented the lack of privacy, the loss of clear identity, and inability to make independent decisions.

Retarded people living outside an institution find ways of accounting for the fact that they were in an institution before.

Some of these reasons given to others for their previous commitment to institutions for the retarded were (1) that their family had abandoned them, (2) that they needed the education that had been provided in the institution, (3) that they had been committed because of a physical illness, or even (4) that they had been committed for criminal acts. None of them wanted to admit that they had been in an institution for the retarded because they were mentally unfit. The message from the studies that have been made of retarded individuals living outside institutions is quite clear: the overwhelming desire of the individual is to be recognized as a competent individual, fit to live in society, a person of worth.

This provides a guiding rule for all programs aimed at helping the retarded adult. Ways must be found to guarantee an adequate level of self-esteem. The stigma of mental retardation must be minimized. The range of successful experiences must be maximized.

The retarded and the law

While it is true that retarded individuals are in trouble with the law no more frequently than others of the same socioeconomic class, what happens to them if they are arrested is often quite different. Their prospects for a speedy trial or a reasonable sentence, if convicted, are much less than for nonretarded individuals.

The retarded person's problems begin at the time of his arrest. First of all, any person arrested for a criminal act must be warned of his legal rights (the Miranda Act). Not only must these warnings be given, but they must be understood for a person to be legally arrested and brought to prosecution. For many of the retarded, it is difficult to know whether the "warning" has been really understood. Moreover, the retarded individual is often afraid of any person in authority. He is motivated to please other people, to appear normal and competent. Therefore, the retarded individual frequently waives his rights when asked to do so by the arresting authorities. He also frequently makes confessions to please the arresting officials. All of these tend to reduce his ability to stay out of custody, whether guilty or innocent.

The next problem concerns a retarded person's competency to stand trial. If the retarded individual's limited mental capacities impair his ability to understand the nature and meaning of a trial, then he is often not brought to trial but committed to some type of state institution. He is judged incompetent to stand trial. In cases of mental illness such a commitment to an institution lasts until the person becomes competent to understand the trial proceedings. How long will this take in the case of the mentally retarded? Many will never understand the meaning of a trial. For them a commitment represents permanent confinement, even for a very minor offense. Experts dealing with the application of our legal system to the retarded have many examples of people who have been permanently confined for very minor crimes. This confinement is ordered without a judgment having been made about the danger posed by the individual to society. His or her punishment is not in proportion to the magnitude of the charged offense. There is no way in which the retarded individual can be released by providing bail, as is done with normal people awaiting trial. The idea of "bail" is based upon establishing a monetary or property deposit that will guarantee that the offender appears for his trial. Yet, if a retarded person is judged incompetent to stand trial, he is indefinitely committed to an institution where he may linger for the rest of his life.

The laws dealing with mental competency are changing in some of the states to make for more sensible handling of people without mental competence. Nevertheless, under the conditions presently existing in almost all of the states, a retarded individual is at a severe disadvantage if suspected of a crime. The punishment can be far beyond the normal limits and, if brought to trial, the retarded person has a substantially greater likelihood of conviction. This is a very serious problem for retarded citizens living in the community on their own or in group-living situations. As more and more retarded individuals live in the community and enjoy the benefits of noninstitutional life, the problem of the retarded and the law will become ever more pressing.

A retarded adult may or may not be judged "incompetent." If not judged incompetent by the appropriate court, a retarded person is able to vote, make contracts, and be responsible for his financial affairs. There are considerable variations in the laws and practices pertaining to the retarded among the fifty states. Parents of the retarded should obtain legal opinions about their children in their own state, for their own benefit as well as for the sake of the retarded individual. The legal opinion is also helpful to the parents in preparing their own wills. Each state has somewhat different rules concerning guardianship, the division of money and property among heirs, and the establishment of trusts. There is no substitute for competent professional advice in these areas.

Programs for the adult

Clearly a wide range of programs must be available to the retarded adult. No single program will be adequate for the needs of all. At one extreme there is the full institutional care which the profoundly retarded obviously require. At the other extreme is the complete freedom of life that some retarded individuals can accept in the community. In between, however, there remains a host of potential programs that may be appropriate to the retarded with different kinds of skills and abilities. For each of them, however, mechanisms of self-fulfillment and self-esteem must be maximized.

Full freedom

The studies of the retarded living on their own in the community reveal a relatively sad picture. Motivated by desires of independence and freedom, dominated by fear of an "institution," these people survive on marginal incomes in apartments, rooms, and "quarters" which are often substandard. They work in jobs unacceptable to nonretarded people and often would fail in society except for the help of people with whom they have accidently established a helpful arrangement on a day-to-day basis. These people need help with grocery shopping, the buying of necessities, transportation, etc. Their freedom is tenuous. To lead fuller lives, these people need to have training in specific skills that would make them more employable in semiskilled or even skilled positions. Therefore, two services are needed:

1 Vocational training appropriate to maintaining a position with higher wages

2 personal counseling appropriate to the management of their most pressing personal difficulties.

The former presents less of a problem in areas where effective vocational rehabilitation programs are available. Moreover, working with vocational rehabilitation training programs does not cast an aura of mental incompetence on the individual, since these programs train people with many kinds of handicaps. Personal counseling need not present a self-esteem problem either, but too often it does, because the services are clearly earmarked only for mentally deficient people. Because of the desire to be considered mentally competent, the retarded are reluctant to use such services. One answer would be to include guidance and counseling services to the retarded as a part of community programs directed toward people with handicaps of any kind. This would not single out the retarded in any special way.

Supervised living-foster homes

Many retarded individuals can be employed and engage in normal community activities if minimal living conditions are provided. These include room and board. Sometimes these are provided by the family, but this need not be the best means of providing the minimal support which a retarded individual requires. Frequently, the family is too supportive and too protective for the person to reach a full measure of independence. More and more, state and federal funds are being used to contract for room and board services for the retarded in homes in the community. Supervision of these foster homes is provided by the state. The retarded person is employed, goes to his job daily, handles most, if not all, of his personal affairs, and yet has a reasonable "home base." From his wages he pays a substantial portion of the costs of his housing and food in the foster home. The fundamental problem to be overcome, once again, is the identification of this arrangement as one uniquely prepared for a person with inadequate mental competencies.

In some states foster-home living is associated with almost complete independence from the facilities and services available to the retarded living in institutions. Sometimes those living in foster homes are not allowed to use medical and dental services for the retarded. This is a difficult problem, to be sure; the fact is that the logic and mechanics of annual physical examinations and health insurance often are beyond these people's mental abilities. This highlights the need for continued supervision and guidance and for access to health care services when needed.

Supervised group-living homes

State and federal funds are now being used to provide housing and food for small groups (five to twenty) of people who live together outside an institution under the direction of "house parents." These group-living situations are often thought of as transitional living arrangements between institutions and full independence. Room and board are provided. The residents are employed in the community. They buy their own clothes, are encouraged to begin saving their money, learn how to get around the community, and are more or less responsible for their own rooms and personal belongings. They contribute to their support from their wages.

The degree to which a retarded person can succeed in the community can be evaluated while he is in a group-living situation. If the person shows that he can manage his job, his social life, and his finances adequately, he is often moved from there to a foster home or "released" to full independence in the community.

Yet, as we have noted above, the group-living situation suffers from the fact that it brings together individuals who all share the same handicap; they are all mentally retarded. This creates a situation in which the house where they live represents the assignment of a social stigma. Neighbors, residents in the area, and others know that a person lives there because he is mentally limited. This is the very stigma the retarded person is trying to avoid. It remains for the designers of community programs to find ways in which this symbol of retardation can be eliminated in the future.

Institutional living with outside employment

For many years some of the retarded living in institutions have worked "outside." Jobs in the community have been found for some of the residents of the institutions. Each day many leave the grounds to work. This is becoming even more commonplace today as a first step in moving a person from institution-based to outside living. If a person is competent to hold employment outside an institution, it is likely that he also will be competent to survive in the community in a foster home or a group-living program. Therefore, employment beyond the confines of an institution probably represents the first test of an individual's capacities to function in society and one which will quickly lead to residential placement outside the institution.

On releasing people from institutions

As mentioned earlier, much of the pressure directed toward releasing people from institutions is based as much upon economics as upon the desire to help the individual reach his fullest potential. In many cases there is ample justification for releasing residents to allow them to lead fuller lives, but often zeal for emptying the institutions overcomes a careful, considered evaluation of the capacities of the particular retarded individual.

When should a retarded individual be released from an institution into the community? Complete release from an institution or from supervision should only occur when the retarded person can be expected to lead a full and rich life. This depends upon two sets of factors: (1) the characteristics of the individual and (2) the circumstances and opportunities in the community.

The individual leaving the institution should have the capacities and prior training to be able to profit from community-based educational, vocational, and habilitation programs. Furthermore, the person should not have characteristics which make community living difficult; for example, chronic illnesses, aggressive behaviors, or uncontrollable seizures. Also, community services must exist for the individual to profit from them. If appropriate education, vocational training, or even jobs are not available, there is little reason to send the person beyond the institution. Beyond these immediate considerations, however, permanent placement outside of the institution should only be considered when the retarded person is able to find and maintain a good job and, furthermore, *is capable of promotion into higher-level jobs*. They should be able to find employment at least at the minimum wage under decent circumstances, that is, circumstances which are acceptable to nonretarded individuals. Beyond concerns about employment, retarded individuals released from institutions should be able to participate in normal recreational activities. They should have the ability to engage in normal sexual activities and to conform to the accepted sexual practices of the community. They should be evaluated for potential genetic transmission of abnormalities to their offspring and be able to undertake marriage and the rearing of children.

Another aspect of normal life is citizenship. A retarded individual living independently in the community should be able to indicate his concern over community and national affairs through verbal expression and the use of the ballot.

Individuals released on their own cognizance should be capable of looking ahead to the future. They should be able to understand that medical and dental hygiene are important and that these cost money. They should be able to anticipate medical costs and to understand the nature of insurance. It is important for them to be able to provide for their dependents. They must also be able to anticipate the effects of their actions upon other people, including obeying laws and regulations, but beyond this to understanding how their actions affect those around them.

Unless the individuals are capable of these functions, it is an injustice to release them from institutions or from adequate and continuing supervision. It is most likely that an individual may function in some of these realms but not in others. Under such circumstances individuals should have continuing ties to, and assistance from, appropriate state agencies. They should be engaged in individualized programs that allow them to exercise their abilities so far as possible. Guidance and direction must be provided where needed.

Community-based programs must work in conjunction with institutions to provide an enriched life for those who must have some association with an institution indefinitely.

Many community-based programs offer substantial hope for improving the lives of the retarded. All programs need to be improved to allow people suffering from mental retardation to live to their fullest potential. Improved programs can only come about through the combined efforts of many individuals. These personal efforts can take many forms, but perhaps the most important of all is the use of imagination in the developing of new approaches to the problems faced by the retarded. If the ideas are worthwhile, ways of implementing them can be found at local, regional, and national levels.

Unfortunately, the needs of the retarded have not been placed very high in the priority of most societies in the past. Consequently, they have been neglected to a considerable degree. There are signs that this historic neglect is changing to concern, and concern is becoming action in many parts of the world. It is to be hoped that actions undertaken to improve the lot of the retarded will be coordinated with actions taken to improve the living conditions of all mankind.

APPENDIX
Suggested books for parents of retarded children

Battin, R. Ray, and Haug, C. Olaf. *Speech and Language Delay: A Home Training Program.* 2d ed. Springfield, Ill.: Charles C Thomas, Publisher, 1968.

Bernstein, Bebe. *Everyday Problems and the Child with Learning Difficulties.* New York: John Day Company, 1967.

Blanton, Elsie. *A Helpful Guide in Training of a Mentally Retarded Child.* New York: National Association for Retarded Children, Publication No. H28. 1968.

Cruikshank, William M. *The Brain-Injured Child in Home, School and Community.* Syracuse, N.Y.: Syracuse University Press, 1967.

Ecob, Katharine G. *Deciding What's Best for Your Retarded Child.* New York: Mental Health Materials Center, Inc., 1956.

Edgerton, Robert B. *The Cloak of Competence: Stigma in the Lives of the Mentally Retarded.* Berkeley: University of California Press, 1967.

Egg, Maria. *Educating the Child Who Is Dif-*

ferent. New York: John Day Company, 1968.

French, Edward L., and Scott, J. Clifford. *How You Can Help Your Retarded Child.* Philadelphia: J. B. Lippincott Company, 1967.

Gaver, J. R. *Birth Defects and Your Baby.* New York: Lancer Books, 1972.

Hunt, Nigel. *The World of Nigel Hunt: The Diary of a Mongoloid Youth.* New York: Garrett Publications, 1967.

Katz, Elias. *The Retarded Adult in the Community.* Springfield, Ill.: Charles C Thomas, Publisher, 1968.

Kirk, Samuel A.; Karnes, Merle B.; and Dirk, Winifred D. *You and Your Retarded Child: A Manual for Parents of Retarded Children.* Palo Alto, Calif.: Pacific Books, 1968.

Levinson, Abraham. *The Mentally Retarded Child.* Rev. ed. New York: John Day Company, 1965.

McDonald, Eugene T. *Understanding Those Feelings.* Pittsburgh: Stanwix House, Inc., 1962.

Murray, Dorothy G. *Needs of Parents of Mentally Retarded Children.* New York: National Association for Retarded Children, Publication No. H97. 1968.

Schimke, R. Neil. *Inheritance and Mental Retardation.* New York: National Association for Retarded Children, Publication No. H50. 1968.

Seagoe, May V. *Yesterday Was Tuesday, All Day and All Night*. Boston: Little, Brown & Company, 1964.

Spock, Benjamin, and Lerrigo, Marion O. *Caring for Your Disabled Child*. New York: Macmillan Company, 1965.

U.S. Government Printing Office. *Feeding the Child with a Handicap*. Washington, D.C.: Children's Bureau, Publication No. 430. 1967.